Land Supply Monitoring

Books from the Lincoln Institute of Land Policy/OG&H

Land Acquisition in Developing Countries
Michael G. Kitay

Introduction to Computer Assisted Valuation
Edited by Arlo Woolery and Sharon Shea

Second World Congress on Land Policy, 1983
Edited by Matthew Cullen and Sharon Woolery

The Zoning Game Revisited
Richard F. Babcock and Charles L. Siemon

Advanced Industrial Development
Donald Hicks

**Land Markets and Land Policy in a Metropolitan Area: A Case
Study of Tokyo**
Yuzuru Hanayama

The Urban Caldron
Edited by Joseph DiMento, LeRoy Graymer, and Frank Schnidman

Land Readjustment: The Japanese System
Luciano Minerbi, Peter Nakamura, Kiyoko Nitz, and Jane Yanai

Measuring Fiscal Capacity
Edited by H. Clyde Reeves

Economics and Tax Policy
Karl E. Case

A Redefinition of Real Estate Appraisal Precepts and Processes
Edited by William N. Kinnard, Jr.

Land Supply Monitoring

A Guide for Improving Public and Private Urban Development Decisions

David R. Godschalk
Scott A. Bollens
John S. Hekman
Mike E. Miles
University of North Carolina
Chapel Hill

A Lincoln Institute of Land Policy Book

Published by
Oelgeschlager, Gunn & Hain
in association with the
Lincoln Institute of Land Policy

International Standard Book Number: 0-89946-211-1

Library of Congress Catalog Card Number: 85-31079

Printed in the U.S.A.

Oelgeschlager, Gunn & Hain, Publishers, Inc.
131 Clarendon Street
Boston, MA 02116

Library of Congress Cataloging-in-Publication Data
Main entry under title:
Land supply monitoring.
  "A Lincoln Intitute of Land Policy book."
  Bibliography: p.
  1. Land use, Urban—Data processing. 2. City planning. I. Godschalk, David R.
II. Lincoln Institute of Land Policy.
HD108.15.L36 1986   333.77'11'0285574   85-31079
ISBN 0-89946-211-1

Contents

Foreword

All who are concerned about the high cost of housing will benefit from this report. It focuses on the land component of urban development, targeting a vital need for accurate information on buildable lands for housing and other urban needs. The report provides a first time summary of how a number of local governments monitor their supply of buildable lands, sets forth guidelines on designing such systems, and spells out the uses of such information by the public and private sectors. The recommendations are important for the citizen consumer, the private developer, builder, banker, and local official responsible for growth management.

Inattention to the supply issue has resulted in an alarming increase in the cost of land for housing and businesses. Numerous national and local studies show that land costs as a factor of housing costs have risen substantially faster than inflation over the last decade. Land as a percentage of housing costs has increased from a range of 15 to 20 percent to as high as 40% in some markets. Further analyses reveal that continued increases in demand without corollary provisions for supply are driving prices up rapidly and resulting in dislocated growth.

For decades whenever and wherever there was a demand for land for housing, business or farming we almost unhesitatingly organized to finance and build a canal, a plankroad, a railroad, a highway or a sewer or some other facility needed to use land. Under these conditions there was little need to monitor land supplies. Land was plentiful and that fact has been a key factor in the achievement of such national objectives as affordable housing, inexpensive food and reasonably priced services and durable goods.

Times are very different now and supply measurement is crucial. Since 1970 the nation has become concerned with conservation, focusing much more on choices of efficient land uses. Severe constraints on Federal aid for roads or sewers, citizen reluctance to raise local taxes for new services, and, importantly, an insidious philosophy of "I've got mine, I'm not concerned about helping you" have set a stage for an era of relative shortages of buildable lands for new homes and businesses in many regions.

The casual observer might be surprised at this problem statement, for there appears to be plenty of vacant land; but vacant land is not necessarily buildable land given today's requirements. To be suitable for housing, land must meet many criteria—it must be available to a builder, well located, free of severe topographic or sub-soil limitations, approved for use (proper zoning), and serviced with roads and sewers. Buildable land is but a small subset of vacant land and it is heavily dependent on combined public policies and private-market choices.

Today we face a challenge to shape public policies that will assure a supply of buildable lands and preserve the competitive land market. Supplies must be a multiple of demand to forestall inflation yet not so great as to invite irrational and uneconomic patterns of development. These policies can only be defined if local government and the private sector have up-to-date information on the location, amounts and prices of buildable land supplies. This report points the way for the public and private sectors to achieve this goal.

James E. Hoben
Office of Policy Development and
  Research
U.S. Department of Housing and
  Urban Development

Lincoln Institute Foreword

The Lincoln Institute of Land Policy is an educational institute dedicated to the development and exchange of ideas and information pertaining to land policy and property taxation. It is a school offering opportunities for instruction and research. It welcomes government officials, working practitioners, and students to the pursuit of advanced studies.

The Lincoln Institute is also a center for linking the university and the practice of government; for bringing together scholars, professionals, and officials; and for blending the theory and practice of land policy.

One key program area is the examination of the impact of emerging technology on the analysis and implementation of land and tax policy. We have, for a number of years, researched and innovated in the use of computers as tools in both policymaking and program implementation. We have jointly worked with numerous organizations and agencies, including the United States Department of Housing and Urban Development (HUD). It was HUD that provided financial support to the University of North Carolina at Chapel Hill to undertake the study that resulted in the preparation of this book on automated land supply information systems.

Because the scope of this book fits so well within our computerized land management system research effort, we are happy to publish it in our LILP book series. We will also work with HUD, the University of North Carolina at Chapel Hill, and others in further research, and in the implementation of computerized land management systems at the local and state government levels.

Frank Schnidman
Senior Fellow
December 1985

Executive Summary

Our Urban Development Information System was one of the best investments we ever made. Without it, our policy makers never would have been able to keep track of the rapid changes in development and land supply here.

> J. Hamilton Lambert
> County Executive
> Fairfax County, Virginia

The computer information system is an invaluable tool in tracking development activity and competitors, and assures that we are at the leading edge.

> George Walker
> Project Manager, Pacific Scene
> San Diego

Where effective land supply monitoring systems have been set up, people in government and business who are concerned with urban development swear by them. As the above quotes show, both public and private sector decision makers believe that these new systems give them an edge.

High quality supply-side information is the advantage provided by land supply monitoring systems. With these systems, decision makers no longer have to rely on sketchy or outdated reports about land supply conditions. Instead, they have at their fingertips comprehensive and current facts on which to base crucial government and business actions. Now they can coordinate public investments in infrastructure and private investments in urban development projects with present and future supplies of available land. Now they can monitor the impacts of public policies and regulations on the amount and location of developable land and affordable housing. As a consequence, both public and private urban development decisions are greatly improved.

Guidebook Purposes

The purposes of this guidebook are to set forth why we must monitor land supplies and to facilitate the creation of land supply information systems by a broad range of local governments. We seek to do this by providing information about the state of the art in automating land supply information and by deriving guidelines from the experience of current systems for those local governments interested in creating new automated systems.

Recommendations in this guidebook are drawn from an in-depth review of the experience of jurisdictions currently providing land supply information. The review covered the published literature of the field, telephone interviews with the managers and planners of twenty-four systems, and field studies during which we talked with both providers and users of automated land supply information in six areas: Contra Costa County, California; Fairfax County, Virginia; Lane County, Oregon; Montgomery County, Maryland; New Haven, Connecticut; and San Diego, California. Readers will find the case studies particularly helpful in understanding the specific advantages, opportunities, and strategies of providing land supply data.

Why Monitor Land Supply?

Automated land supply information systems (ALSIS) are defined as computerized databases designed to monitor changes in a jurisdiction's land inventory, in order to assist in management and regulation of land development and to facilitate analysis of private market decisions. They enable decision makers to understand the impacts of public policies on the amount, price, and location of land available for development. They enable developers to reduce the risk, uncertainty, and expense of private development projects.

Accurate and timely land supply information can facilitate the provision of affordable housing. Without such information about their local land markets, governments can inadvertently worsen land supply shortages through adopting excessive development regulations and setting overly tight restrictions on the areas designated for urban development. When land supply is overly constrained, development is redirected to less restrictive market areas or land price is inflated. Either way, local housing prices tend to rise.

Two types of jurisdictions will benefit from this guidebook. Areas without a land use information system will learn how to initiate such a system with a strong land supply database. Areas with an existing land use information system will learn how to add more detailed land supply information for use by public and private decision makers.

Jurisdictions that offer accurate and timely land supply information will realize substantial advantages:

- Private development feasibility studies and development proposals based on realistic land supply market data.
- Public land use policies and regulations that account for impacts on land inventories.
- Credible common databases for development feasibility analyses and negotiations between public and private sectors.
- Factual bases for balancing goals of affordable housing, economic development, and orderly growth.
- Improvements in efficiency and effectiveness of administering public programs affecting development, including capital budgeting and infrastructure planning.
- Improvements in quality and timing of private development projects.

State of the Art

Most automated land supply information systems are components of land use information systems operated by local governments. They are relatively new, having been started within the last ten years. The majority use assessor's tax records as a main data source, and add information from building permits, subdivision requests, and Census reports. Increasingly, they are building computer mapping capabilities into their systems. These public systems have enabled governments not only to become more efficient in administering development review and regulation, but also to become more effective in coordinating growth with provision of public facilities.

Alongside the public systems in many areas, private computerized land information services are emerging. The most widespread type of private system is the Multiple Listing Service operated by local realtors associations and providing current information on property for sale. Another important type of private system, operated by real estate and consulting firms, provides real estate and sales data based on government assessment and deed records, supplemented by other sources. Desirable features of these computerized private information services include speedy reporting, areawide market coverage, frequent updating, access by subscription, and custom reports. They enable their clients to stay up to date on the development market and to do more accurate projections and feasibility studies.

The big question for decision makers concerned with land supply is whether or not vacant land in the supply is "developable". In practice, local government information systems have tended to provide information only on a limited set of measurable developability aspects:

- Is the land vacant or underutilized?
- Is it zoned for development?
- Is it provided with urban services?
- Is it free of physical constraints?

Because they do not have complete information or because the questions involve subjective classifications, local governments have tended not to provide information on two further market aspects of developability:

- Is the land available for purchase or development?
- Is it economically feasible to develop?

Recommendations for a Prototype System

The recommended prototype Automated Land Supply Information System (ALSIS) should:

- be organized around the land parcel as its basic unit, with the ability to combine parcel data into subareas such as Census Tracts or planning districts,
- contain information about the existing and forecasted land supply within a jurisdiction, market, or region,
- be accessible to public and private sector users in convenient formats, and
- be designed for monitoring changes in land supply inventory to assist in managing and regulating land development and to facilitate land market analysis.

Recommended features of the prototype ALSIS include data organized into two main files: 1) the "parcel" file with information on individual land parcels, and 2) the "project" file with information on proposed development projects. Three types of data processing organizational options may be used, depending on the local situation: 1) "centralized" systems bring computer equipment and data into a single data processing department, 2) "decentralized" systems locate equipment and data in individual user departments and have no central coordination, and 3) "distributed" systems combine a large central computer with smaller computers in individual departments. The distributed option is recommended, where possible, because of its ability to meet the varying needs of different user departments while also providing central coordination.

Hardware and software decisions should be made in terms of local needs and resources. System development should be seen as a modular process, and should include computer mapping capability when economically feasible. Selection of hardware and software should be based on the jobs to be done by the system, including data storage, database management and access, analysis, report generation, graphics and mapping. Software should be capable of interactive, on-line operation in order to increase data currency and accessibility. Vendor-produced software should be favored over in-house programs.

Capabilities for evaluating land supply can be extended beyond those of current systems. The goal should be a definition of available land supply which is mutually agreed upon by both government and private interests. To refine the classification of developable land within the overall land supply, governments should: 1) conduct surveys of land-owner intentions, 2) subtract current development in process from the estimated available supply, 3) seek to make ALSIS compatible with Multiple Listing Service files, 4) classify vacant land supply by zoning type in each subarea and compare it to subarea demand projections, 5) identify land availability by time periods, based on anticipated public and private actions, 6) include data on recent sales prices and dates, and 7) attempt to improve the accuracy of demand projections.

Implementing an Automated System

Political support is critical to successful adoption of a local land supply information system. Decision makers, public and private, must be convinced of the usefulness of the higher quality information provided by the system in policy formulation, decision support, administration, and development.

A steering committee made up of public and private information users and providers should be formed to guide the design and implementation of the land supply monitoring system. This committee can guide technical work and can enhance support for the new system. Membership should include management level representatives of involved government departments and major private organizations concerned with development, such as the Homebuilders' Association, Realtors' Association, and Chamber of Commerce.

Evaluation of the existing work flows to be automated is a critical task. If the ALSIS is to increase the efficiency and effectiveness of the organization, then it must not build in existing inefficiencies. To gain user department support, the new system should demonstrate its ability to benefit the person with a file in his hand.

Implementation should be staged, with government functions being automated first and then private sector access being incorporated. It is important to show examples of system success early, through such techniques as pilot projects, small scale demonstrations, or enhanced analyses of local problems. Modular design lends itself to staged implementation, particularly through spreading system costs over a number of fiscal years. Staged implementation also reflects the life cycle dynamics of a computerized information system, which will evolve over time as local needs and available technology change.

Acknowledgments

Our main thanks go to the practitioners in the six case study areas who are operating and using land supply information systems. Their patient and generous sharing of their experience and insights enabled us to understand the opportunities and complexities of these systems. We particularly appreciate the help of Bob Nash and Dennis Barry of Contra Costa County, George Kohut of Fairfax County, Jim Carlson and Jim Farah of Lane County, Bob Hnat and Jeff Zyontz of Montgomery County, Daniel Kops and Gerardo Canto of New Haven, and Tim O'Connell of San Diego.

Jim Hoben of HUD, our Government Technical Representative, played a major role throughout our study. His vision of the need for land supply information as a contributor to the achievement of affordable housing informed the project's social purpose. His concern for bringing the public and private sectors together in collaborative information systems informed the project's research strategy.

Review comments on the draft report were received from Richard Brail of Rutgers University; David Dowall of the University of California at Berkeley; Tony Ahuja of the Northern Virginia Builders Association, and Frank Schnidman, Dennis Robinson, Alven Lam, and Mat MacIver of the Lincoln Institute of Land Policy. We appreciate their constructive suggestions, which helped to improve the final report.

Many others assisted in the study. Information system managers and planning directors from the twenty-four jurisdictions provided useful information about the operational and policy aspects of their systems. Those who have written about land supply information issues were helpful in orienting our efforts, and we have recognized their publications in the text. We are grateful to all whose knowledge is drawn upon here.

I

Land Supply Information and the Development Process

The purposes of this guidebook are to establish the need for, and to describe the status of, automated land supply information systems, and to recommend guidelines for local governments seeking to establish such systems. Automated land supply information systems are computerized databases designed to monitor changes in a jurisdiction's land inventory, to assist in management and regulation of land development, and to facilitate analysis of private market decisions.

Two types of jurisdictions will benefit from this guidebook. First, jurisdictions without a computerized land use information system will find recommendations on how to initiate such a system with a strong land supply database. Second, jurisdictions that already have conventional, computerized land use or geographic information systems will learn how to include more detailed land supply information for use by public and private decision makers.

Local governments, developers, lending institutions, and other real estate professionals need land supply information to ensure effective land management and development processes. A growing number of public and private computer-based systems have been set up to monitor development and provide land market data. These systems, feasible because of advances in computer technology, are powerful policy and decision analysis tools.

Complete analysis of a local land market requires information on the interaction between the supply of land and the demand for land. While this guide focuses on land supply information, particularly residential land supply information, we recognize the importance of demand projection and analysis in the determination of the adequacy of local land supply.

A. Informing Land Policy and Market Decisions

We would find it impossible to keep up with growth demands without our Urban Development Information System. For example, our permit section is processing 37% more permits today. The system's benefits penetrate all levels of government, making our work faster and more efficient. Uses are growing daily.

George Kohut
Fairfax County, Virginia

Land supply information is the "missing link" in many critical local development decisions. Public policies regulating the amount of land available for development made without benefit of accurate land inventory knowledge can have disastrous effects on the price of raw land or the efficiency of providing public facilities. Private development decisions made without timely knowledge about land supply in the local market can drive up housing costs unnecessarily. Such imperfect information multiplies the risk and uncertainty of both public and private development decisions.

Risk and uncertainty make development more expensive. The consumer pays more for housing since higher risk projects require higher investor returns. Market uncertainty limits competition and forces the developer to pay more for land if the market is artificially constrained. The government pays more for public facilities when they are not properly sized due to uncertain knowledge about the actual supply of land available for development. As each decision maker adds "safety factors" to compensate for missing information, affordable housing possibilities shrink.

Land use policies and regulations based on solid land supply information can encourage affordable housing. Land price is a significant and growing proportion of housing costs, which have risen rapidly in recent years. (Black and Hoben, 1984; Seidel, 1978) Because land prices are sensitive to supply as well as demand, local policies on land use regulation, infrastructure provision, and tax rates can have important housing cost effects. (Dowall, 1984) A 1977 ULI study found that 20-30% of San Jose housing cost increases resulted from public growth policies. These policies influence both the economics of private development and the availability of public services, key factors in the supply of land for development. Improved land supply information allows public officials to give proper consideration to the market impacts of development restrictions and incentives. (Dowall and Mingilton, 1979) For example, some growth management programs build in a market factor, an extra land supply beyond projected demand, to lessen the effect of supply constraints. (Portland MSD, 1979; Metro Council, 1975; San Diego, 1985)

Overestimation of the supply of land available for development can lead to increased land prices and, consequently, increased housing costs, when public policy does not allow the true supply to expand to meet demand. (Segal and Srinivasan, 1980) Poor land supply information can cause see-saw swings in public policy, generating uncertainty about government intentions and defeating efforts at public-private cooperation. Lack of understanding of market conditions can deflect growth to neighboring jurisdictions, and can open public decision makers to legal challenges if local growth management regulations are judged exclusionary.

Governments that seek to influence the location, timing, and amount of growth within their jurisdictions have been characterized as "managing a market, not implementing a physical design." (Einsweiler, 1979) This is because their development management programs should be seeking to balance market supply and demand dynamics, rather than to carry out an end-state spatial plan. To do this effectively, they must monitor land supply so they can periodically adjust their forecasts of urban space and facility needs.

Unless they understand market dynamics, governments can cause land supply shortages through adopting excessive development regulations, causing needless delays in reviewing development proposals, and setting overly tight restrictions on the size of areas designated for urban development. When land supply is constrained, development is redirected to less restrictive market areas or land price is inflated. (Dowall, 1981) Either way, local housing prices tend to rise.

Advantages of access to accurate and timely residential land supply information include:

- Private development feasibility studies and development proposals based on realistic land supply market data.
- Public land use policies and regulations that account for impacts on land inventories.
- Credible common databases for development feasibility analyses and negotiations between public and private sectors.
- Factual bases for balancing goals of affordable housing, economic development, and orderly growth.
- Improvements in efficiency and effectiveness of administering public programs affecting development.
- Improvements in quality and timing of private development projects.

B. Land Development Actors and Information Needs

Each actor in the complex chain of decisions necessary to develop a residential project needs land supply information. For the development process to best serve each actor's needs, this information should be consistent between, and accessible to, both public and private sectors.

Public sector development actors need land supply and demand information to prepare and update comprehensive plans, to design zoning and other development regulations, to program capital improvements and public infrastructure, and to administer development management programs. Without accurate data on the existing supply, current change, and future forecast of land available for development, public officials are "flying blind" in their decision making. Land supply inventories and forecasts should include information on location, amount, and characteristics of land, relationship to capacities of public services and critical areas, and changes due to development in the "pipeline" (approved or underway but not occupied).

From initial project idea inception through construction, private sector development actors also use supply and demand data. (Graaskamp, 1985) Their need for land supply data is most pressing in the stage of investigating project feasibility, when they analyze the land supply inventory both as a market basket of potential sites and as a set of competing projects and products. At this stage they need to know as much as possible about land availability, ownership, price, zoning and other regulatory use restrictions, and relationships to other existing and proposed development. (Wurtzebach and Miles, 1984; Graaskamp, 1970) The same type of information is needed if they are seeking rezoning or other development regulation approvals. As they move into the design and site plan approval stage, they need more detailed information about land characteristics (soils, slope, vegetation, etc.), available services (roads, water, sewer, etc.), and specific public development regulatory requirements.

Types of Land Supply Information Needs

Government Actors	Concerns
Elected officials	Public policy and land supply issues and impacts
Planners	Land supply/demand, services, critical areas, growth patterns

Tax assessors	Land use, value, amount, characteristics
Engineers	Public facility provision, capacity, location
Building inspectors	Status and characteristics of development projects
Private Sector Actors	*Concerns*
Realtors, appraisers, consultants, information services	Land availability, ownership, price, use potential, development activity
Land assemblers and developers	Status of land market, zoning and regulations, facilities/services
Homebuilders	Developed sites and submarkets
Engineers, architects, site planners	Land characteristics, services, regulations
Lenders	Feasibility of proposed projects

C. New Opportunities for Monitoring Land Supply

When the early computerized land information systems were created, there was no perceived need for land supply monitoring. Also, the equipment was too expensive, the technical skills too demanding, and the state-of-the-art too undeveloped to permit widespread adoption of these innovative systems. Early information automation often occurred in independent efforts, spurred by transportation planning, Census Bureau programs such as the DIME Files, and advances in geographic base files and printer mapping technology. (Horwood, 1980)

Today, the need is clear, and the technology and knowledge necessary for computerized land information systems are available to a broad range of local governments. Computers have gained an accepted role in local government. (Dueker, 1980; Huxhold, 1981; Kraemer, 1981) Mass production of computers has reduced the price, major increases in computing speed and data capacity have upgraded the capacity of smaller machines, commercial marketing of standard software packages has decreased the need for in-house programming, and diffusion of lessons from the experience of the pioneers in the field has clarified the underlying principles necessary for effective operations. (Stern and Stern, 1985)

Coupled with recent advances in computer communications systems and in both public and private sector understanding of the use of computer databases for decision making, these new technological developments suggest an emerging era of computerized land records systems with powerful land supply monitoring capabilities. This guidebook studies the experience of a current group of such systems to develop guidelines for local governments desiring to participate in this new era.

D. Study Approach

In order to document the experience of jurisdictions currently providing land supply information with computerized land record systems, three investigations were conducted. First, we reviewed the literature describing and analyzing land information systems. Second, we did a telephone reconnaissance of those systems identified in the literature that monitored land supply, particularly in relation to fringe area growth and development policy. Third, we conducted field studies of six automated systems actively oriented toward tracking vacant land, in order to talk with system users as well as information providers.

To derive guidelines and recommendations for designing and implementing automated land supply monitoring as part of a land use information system, we followed a three step process. First, we abstracted elements of a prototype system from the literature and organized them as tentative guidelines. Second, we tested our tentative prototype in interviews with experienced system providers and users during the six individual case studies. Third, we expanded, revised, and reformulated the guidelines on the basis of our aggregate learning from the case studies.

The four chapters of this report are organized around the assumption that the reader will want to know first "why" to consider initiating a land supply information system, second "what" current public and private information systems look like, third "how" to design an automated land supply information system, and fourth "who" should be involved in the stages of system implementation. The first two chapters describe the state of the art; the last two make recommendations for setting up new systems. Material in these chapters is presented in the form of overall findings and guidelines. For readers seeking more detail, the appendices contain reports on the six case studies (Contra Costa County, California; Fairfax County, Virginia; Lane County, Oregon; Montgomery County, Maryland; New Haven, Connecticut; and San Diego, California), brief descriptions of the twenty-four public systems contacted in the telephone reconnaissance, and an annotated bibliography from the literature review. Finally, a glossary of computer information terms is provided at the end of this report.

II

Current Land Information Systems

The computerized information system has been like magic . . . a great management and planning tool.

Larry Gunn
Building Inspection Department
Contra Costa County

This chapter examines existing land information systems and discusses the major issues involved in land information provision. First, the results of a telephone reconnaissance of 24 monitoring jurisdictions are discussed. Second, we briefly review several emerging private land information systems. Third, the important topic of assessing land developability is discussed, focusing especially on the problems of determining the amount of "available" or "economically feasible" land supply. Finally, we identify a number of major land information provision issues.

A. Existing Public Systems

Existing public land information systems with land supply tracking elements record the following types of parcel-specific information: physical constraints, density potential based on zoning, and public actions such as subdivisions and rezonings. They commonly use mainframe computers; however, most systems initiated since 1980 are microcomputer-based. The most common data source is the tax assessor's records, and the basic unit of tabulation is the tax parcel.

Comprehensive updating of the information system database is typically done annually.

Jurisdictions vary in their definitions of the types of vacant land. The adjectives "developable" and "constrained" are commonly used in describing vacant land. However, "developable" is not defined from a private sector perspective by looking at what areas and parcels are actually or potentially for sale and suitable for a marketable project.

To explore the current state of the art in local public land information systems, we identified twenty-four (24) jurisdictions which either currently have a land information system (19), are developing one (3), or have had a system in the past (2). These systems were identified through two primary sources: the literature review (see the Annotated Bibliography) and the telephone reconnaissance. Not all existing land supply information systems were examined in this study. Indeed, one of the interesting findings of the phone survey is that many land information systems are little known outside of their own jurisdictions. However, we feel that this survey of existing public systems is a representative treatment of current land supply information systems.

Our focus during the telephone reconnaissance was on monitoring jurisdictions with large amounts of vacant land within and on the fringe of their jurisdictional limits. Intentionally bypassed in the phone survey were those monitoring systems in built-up urban areas oriented toward identifying infill opportunities (one exception, the New Haven monitoring system, was included in the phone survey and as a case study for comparative purposes). The infill monitoring systems can more accurately be labeled as "vacant lot inventories" rather than "land supply information systems". Their mission is to identify development opportunities on individual parcels rather than assist in obtaining an overall picture of land supply relative to demand. Vacant lot inventories exist in cities such as Toledo, Milwaukee, Wilmington (DE), Alexandria (VA), Boston, Pittsburgh, Cincinnati and Cleveland. For information on vacant lot inventories, refer to the Real Estate Research Corporation report listed in the annotated bibliography.

The operational head of the land information system in each of the 24 jurisdictions was interviewed by telephone using a standardized questionnaire. For approximately one-third of the jurisdictions, a second call to a policy official (usually the planning director) was made to obtain additional information.

Comparative information on the 24 systems examined is presented in Tables A, B, and C. The information collected for each system appears as the column headings. Tables A and B generally describe the components of each system, while Table C focuses on types of information collected on vacant land. What follows is an overview of the predominant characteristics and contrasts of the 24 systems. For information on any specific system, the reader is referred to Appendix B (Characteristics of 24 Public Land Supply Information Systems).

Regional Location of Jurisdiction: Based on the Bureau of the Census regional breakdown of states, thirteen (13) land supply information systems studied are in the West, eight (8) are in the South, two (2) are in the North Central region, and one (1) is located in the Northeast. Land supply information systems in our reconnaissance are predominantly located in the growing Western and Southern regions, illustrating the linkage between monitoring systems and high-growth areas. It should be kept in mind, however, that the telephone survey was not a random sample, and that such conclusions are tentative. Fully one-third of the 24 monitoring systems studied are located in California, a state that now requires jurisdictions to include an inventory of land resources in their Housing Elements. The two systems in the North Central region are in the Minneapolis and Dayton, Ohio areas; the one system in the Northeast is located in New Haven, Connecticut and is oriented toward identifying infill opportunities for housing, commercial, and industrial development.

Year Started: The recency of land supply information systems is brought out in the following breakdown of surveyed systems by start-up year:

Before 1975:   4
1975-1979:   10
1980 and after: 10

Type of System: Mainframe oriented systems are still predominant among surveyed systems, as the following breakdown of the 24 jurisdictions shows:

Mainframe: 11
Microcomputer: 6
Linked (mainframe-micro or mini-micro):   3
Minicomputer: 2
Manual: 2

This mainframe orientation seems to be decreasing in systems developed in 1980 or after. Five of the 10 systems with start-up dates in 1980 or after are microcomputer based, and two systems are linked (one is mainframe-micro linked and the other is mini-micro linked).

Table A
System Descriptions
Survey of Land Information Systems

Jurisdiction Name	Year Started	Type of System	Main Users	Main Data Source
Association of Bay Area Governments (ABAG)	1976	Manual	Internal (and member cities)	Local govt. records, maps
Charlotte	In development	Mainframe	Private interests	Tax records
Contra Costa County, CA	1982	Main-micro link	Internal, private	Tax records, individual agency data
Dallas	1979/1980	Mainframe	Private interests	Tax records
Denver	1970	Main-micro link	Internal	Tax records
Fairfax County, VA	1972/73	Mainframe	Internal, private, and elected	Tax records, 6 other sources
Houston	1983	Interactive graphing system, minicomputer	Internal (other agencies)	Tax records, aerial photos
Jacksonville, FL	In development	Microcomputer	Internal, elected, private	Building permits, tax records
King County, WA	1977	Mainframe	Private, internal and elected officials	Tax records
Lane County, OR	1970	Mainframe	Internal, private	Tax records
Los Angeles	Mid-1970's	Mainframe	Internal (some private)	Tax records

Location	Year	System	Users	Data sources
Miami Valley, (Ohio) Regional Planning Council	1975	Mainframe	Elected, internal	Aerial photos
Minneapolis	1980	Manual (currently being automated)	Internal, elected, and private	Aerial photos (tax records in future)
Montgomery County, MD	1980	Mini-micro	Internal, private	Tax records
New Haven	1984	Micro	Internal mainly	Tax records, Dime files
Phoenix	1980	Manual, with plans to automate to micro	Internal (some elected, private)	Maps, field surveys (bldg. permits in future)
Portland Metro	1977	Micro	Internal	Land use maps
Sacramento	In development	Micro	Internal, elected	Tax records
San Diego	1975	Mainframe	Internal, private, elected	Tax records
San Jose	1977	Mini	Internal	Aerial photos
Santa Clara County, CA	1984	Micro	Internal	Tax records, Dime files
Stockton	1968	Mainframe	Internal	Field surveys, bldg. permit data
Tulsa	1977/1978 (discontinued)	Mainframe	Internal, private	Tax records, bldg. permits
Washington, DC (MAGIS)	1976	Mainframe	Internal, private, and elected	Tax records, 5 other sources

Table B
System Descriptions *(cont.)*
Survey of Land Information Systems

Jurisdiction Name	Basic Unit of Tabulation	Updating	Qualifiers Attached to Vacant Land Definition
Association of Bay Area Governments (ABAG)	Census tract	1981–1982	Available according to local plans
Charlotte	Parcel	Annually (forecasted)	Subdivided (yes and no), under construction
Contra Costa County, CA	Parcel	Day-to-day	None
Dallas	Parcel	1980	None
Denver	Parcel	Annually	Developable (qualitative studies)
Fairfax County, VA	Parcel	Tax records annually, permits daily	Underutilized
Houston	Parcel	Once/year	None
Jacksonville, FL	Traffic analysis zones	Unknown at this time	Developable (not in wetlands)
King County, WA	½ section (approx. ½ sq. mile)	Weekly/quarterly	Constrained and unconstrained
Lane County, OR	Parcel	Annually	Developable, buildable

City	Geographic unit	Update frequency	Vacant land classification
Los Angeles	Parcel	Every 6 months	None
Miami Valley (Ohio) Regional Planning Council	Various, not parcel specific	None	Available based on land capability analysis
Minneapolis	Digitized polygon (in future)	1984 (every 4 years)	Vacant–restrained
Montgomery County, MD	Parcel, census tract	Parcel file quarterly, subdivision file daily	Partially vacant, farm assessed
New Haven	Parcel	Weekly, every 6 months	Back taxes, liens
Phoenix	Traffic analysis zones	1982	Developable, land reserved
Portland Metro	Census tract	1980, 1983	Vacant–with hazard
Sacramento	Parcel, census tract	Unknown at this time	Vacant–constrained
San Diego	Parcel	Day-to-day	None
San Jose	Digitized polygon	Annually	Within urban services area
Santa Clara County, CA	Parcel	Annually (forecasted)	None
Stockton	Census tract	Annually	None
Tulsa	Parcel	None	Constrained
Washington, DC (MAGIS)	Parcel	Annually	Truly vacant, falsely vacant

Two of the three systems currently being developed are micro based. For the 10 systems developed in 1980 and after, the breakdown is as follows:

Mainframe:	1
Microcomputer:	5
Linked (mainframe-micro or mini-micro):	2
Minicomputer:	1
Manual:	1

Main Data Source: Seventeen of the 24 land information systems are tied into assessor's tax records. Other main data sources include building permit, subdivision information, and Census information. As automation of land information systems increases, the use of aerial photos as a primary data source has decreased. Only three of the surveyed jurisdictions now use aerial photos as a primary data source.

Basic Unit of Tabulation: As displayed in Table B, fifteen of the 24 surveyed systems use the tax parcel as the basic unit of tabulation. Other units used as the basic unit include Census Tracts and traffic analysis zones.

Updating: The frequency of updating of the database varies across systems. Although computer technology exists which can allow more frequent updating, most systems are still updated on a yearly basis. The breakdown is as follows:

At intervals greater than 1 year:	5
Annually:	9
Weekly/quarterly/biannually:	3
Daily:	3
Other (includes "not known yet" and "no updating"):	4

Three systems—Tulsa, Miami Valley, and Dallas—have not been updated and are thus one-time inventories. The first two of these jurisdictions have discontinued their systems due to the cost of updating the database.

Qualifiers Attached to Vacant Land Definition: Jurisdictions vary in their definitions of different types of vacant land. One-third of the jurisdictions make no attempt to define "developable" or "buildable" vacant land. These jurisdictions, instead, collect information on vacant land and let the user of the system's information define what is developable or not from his viewpoint.

Most of the jurisdictions which attempt to define developability levels of vacant land do so on the basis of physical hazard constraints, especially slope and floodplain constraints. "Developable" is frequently used to describe vacant lands not constrained by physical hazards, while "constrained" is often used to describe physically encumbered vacant parcels.

No jurisdictions surveyed make an attempt to define "developability" from the private sector perspective by identifying areas and parcels actually or potentially for sale. Many of the surveyed jurisdictions told of the difficulties involved when government attempts to define developability on the basis of market availability and/or economic feasibility of development. The subjective and time-dependent nature of such a definition led many jurisdictions to define developability mainly on the basis of the absence of physical limitations.

Information Collected on Vacant Land: Table C contains specific information on the kinds of land supply information collected on vacant land. The following breakdown shows the number of systems which collect the listed type of information:

Number of surveyed systems: 24

Public service availability:	9
Physical limits/constraints:	12
Density potential/zoning:	16
Previous sales price:	6
Forecasted time of development:	3

Land information systems commonly track public decisions regarding vacant land parcels. This information is frequently referred to as the administrative history of a parcel. The following breakdown shows the number of systems which track the listed type of public decision:

Number of surveyed systems: 24

Annexations:	14
Subdivisions:	14
Rezonings:	15
Infrastructure decisions:	7

Computer Mapping Capabilities: The last column of Table C shows whether computerized mapping is part of the land information system. Six of the 24 systems currently have computer mapping capabilities, with three more jurisdictions planning to have such capabilities in the near future.

Table C
Information Collected on Vacant Land
Survey of Land Information Systems

Jurisdiction Name	Public Service Availability	Physical Limits	Density Potential	Sales Price	Subdivisions	Rezonings	Graphics/ Mapping Capability
ABAG	xx		xx			xx	
Charlotte	xx	xx	xx		xx	xx	
Contra Costa	xx		xx		xx	xx	
Dallas	xx						
Denver			xx	xx	xx	xx	
Fairfax			xx	xx	xx	xx	In future
Houston			N/A		xx	N/A	xx
Jacksonville							
King County		xx	xx		xx	xx	

Lane County	xx	xx	xx	xx	xx	xx
Los Angeles		xx		xx	xx	In future
Miami Valley		xx				xx
Minneapolis		xx				In future
Montgomery	xx	xx	xx	xx	xx	
New Haven		xx	xx	xx	xx	xx
Phoenix		xx		xx	xx	
Portland		xx			xx	
Sacramento		xx		xx	xx	
San Diego		xx		xx	xx	
San Jose	xx	xx				xx
Santa Clara County	xx					xx
Stockton		xx		xx	xx	
Tulsa	xx					
Washington, DC			xx			

B. Emerging Private Systems

We find that almost everyone in the real estate community has a valid need for current comparables on all types of property, including vacant land.

> California Market Data Cooperative, Inc.
> Glendale, California

Land information is provided by private organizations as well as governments. The most widespread type of private land information system is the Multiple Listing Service operated by local associations of realtors across the country. A 1983 national survey of real estate firms found 34% of those surveyed had access to a computerized Multiple Listing Service. (National Association of Realtors, 1984) Private information systems, increasingly automated, play a major role in providing data about land price and availability and about links between the supply and demand functions of land markets.

During our case study visits to six selected areas with public land information systems, we discovered several private land information systems in operation. Able to move faster than governments in computerizing and selling data from public records and other sources, these private systems are increasingly part of the land information network. Because they raise important issues for governments desiring to operate land information systems, these private systems are briefly discussed here.

Eight private land information services were found, ranging from online remote terminal systems to systems producing various types of periodically published listings. They covered jurisdictions located in the Washington, D.C. metropolitan area and in California. Six of the services delivered information on real estate listings and comparable sales; one focused on land use and development potential, and one tracked applications for and actions on development in the pipeline. All utilized computers, but only two delivered information to the consumer via remote terminal. The services included:

Selected Private Land Information Services

NAME	*LOCATION*	*OUTPUT*
Montgomery County MLS	Kensington MD	Online real estate listings

LUSKNET	Washington D.C.	Online real estate data
LandTrak	San Francisco	Development potential reports
Sager Documaster	Woodbridge VA	Real estate microfiche
Moholt Data Service	Gaithersburg MD	Comparable sales data
Cal. Market Data Coop.	Glendale CA	Comparable sales data
Call-COMPS	Southern CA	Comparable sales data
Fairfax Newsletter	Reston VA	Building permits, zoning, plats

The Montgomery County Board of Realtors computerized Multiple Listing Service is an online database in which some 5,000 users operate from about 1,100 terminals to both read out and enter data on resale of property within the County. Data entered from remote terminals is cross checked by the central office staff against written listings. A continuous training program is operated for members using the system. The system uses software designed inhouse on IBM Series 1 hardware, which can communicate with 120 terminals at a time.

LUSKNET functions as an online computer data bank, in which subscribers have access through remote terminals in their offices over telephone lines. Operated by a Washington real estate information service, Rufus S. Lusk & Son, Inc., LUSKNET provides dial-up access to continuously updated databases of real estate sales and tax assessment information for the Washington metropolitan area. Data is gathered from county assessors and deed recorders. Users, such as appraisers and development consultants, pay an hourly rate to search the database using keywords to generate custom reports on comparable sales and feasibilty studies.

LandTrak is a database developed by Gruen, Gruen & Associates, a San Francisco consulting firm, to provide their clients with accurate and timely information on land use policy and property development in the Tri-Valley, covering the planning areas of several cities in Alameda and Contra Costa Counties. Development potential is the major concern of the system, which also records parcel data on physical characteristics, demographic links, and jurisdictional and service area location. The system uses Informix relational database management software and a Plexus P/60 super microcomputer.

Sager Inc. operates the Documaster system that provides subscribers with microfiche reports on real estate data in the Washington, D.C. metropolitan area. This system is a compilation of information from assessment records, mortgage records, and land use records. It uses a mainframe computer to convert government computer tapes into microfiche.

The Moholt Data Service provides comparable sales documentation for commercial, industrial, apartment, and land sales in Montgomery County, Maryland. Oriented toward land appraisers, the Service verifies sales at the courthouse and measures and photographs most commercial and industrial sales. Initial reports are furnished in notebooks; telephone modem access is planned.

The California Market Data Cooperative, Inc. of Glendale, California, provides comparable sales data in monthly reports. Members of the coop submit sales information, which is supplemented by sales data from public records. Reports are published monthly.

Call-COMPS is a databank of comparable sales with California offices in San Diego, Orange, Riverside, San Bernardino, and Los Angeles, and an Arizona office in Maricopa. Customers call in and sales representatives assemble real estate data, which is mailed to customers. Monthly reports also are available to subscribers.

The Fairfax Newsletter is a pipeline tracking service that utilizes county data tapes downloaded onto the Newsletter equipment. Published weekly, the Newsletter tracks the Fairfax County development pipeline, reporting actions on building permits, rezonings, site plans, and subdivision plats to some 500 subscribers, including developers, realtors, and builders who need to follow development activities.

From this brief review, it is clear that an increasing number of automated private land supply information services are being created. Except for multiple listing services, these private services typically depend on government information for their base data, but they add such desirable features as speedy reporting, areawide coverage across jurisdictional boundaries, frequent updating, access by subscription, and custom report formating.

C. Assessing Land Developability

In an ideal system oriented toward managing a local residential development market, information would be provided on the amount of vacant land that is "developable", under various definitions (see Figure 1):

1. vacant (with no improvements) or underutilized (improved at less than the density or intensity allowed by zoning or the comprehensive plan),
2. zoned for residential development,
3. provided with urban services, such as water, sewer, and roads,
4. without physical constraints, such as excessive slopes, floodplains, or environmentally sensitive areas,
5. available for purchase or development, and
6. economically feasible to develop.

In practice, local governments tend to provide information only on the first four aspects of land supply. The Association of Bay Area Governments (ABAG) in Oakland, California, has estimated four categories of development potential of vacant land (high, medium, low, and none) based on current local policies and physical hazards. Most jurisdictions that track land use, zoning, infrastructure, and hazards, however, hesitate to declare that certain land is "developable", since that is a partially subjective classification. Steep hillside sites seen as developable in California might not be so judged in North Carolina. They leave the provision of information on land availability and development feasibility, the last two aspects, to private information services and analysts. None of the 24 systems surveyed by our telephone reconnaissance classified developable land in terms of market availability or economic feasibility for development.

Land supply estimates based only on vacant and underutilized classifications, zoning, services, and physical constraints (aspects 1-4) will tend to overestimate the supply of developable land since some of this land will not be on the market or economically feasible to develop. Land supply estimates based only on market availability and feasibility (aspects 5-6) will tend to underestimate the supply of developable land due to incomplete information, uncertainty, and the dynamics of these market dimensions.

Some attempts to incorporate market and feasibility aspects into land information systems have been reported. A Stockton CA study used a stratified random sample of land owners to provide a basis for

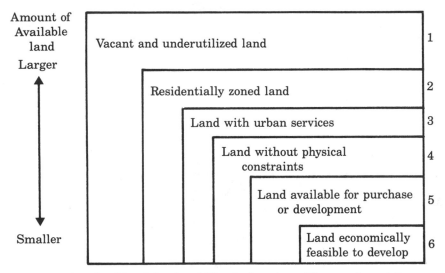

Figure 1. *Levels of land developability for housing. (Figure adapted from People for Open Space, 1983.)*

estimating the vacant, residentially zoned land likely to be available for sale or development between 1980 and 1990. That study evaluated economic feasibility by comparing housing prices in various locations to the costs of producing housing there. It concluded that only 36% of the holding capacity of vacant land designated residential on the Stockton General Plan was likely to be built. (Gruen, Gruen & Associates, 1982) A King County WA study tried to define land availability based on land currently on the market (which understated the potential supply over a 12 year period) and on parcels over five acres in size (which also understated the potential supply since almost half the recent subdivision activity took place on smaller parcels). That study concluded that a definition satisfactory to all public and private parties could not be found. (King County, 1979) Finally, a study of landowner characteristics as determinants of developer locational decisions argued that landowners with low perceived present values for their property were most likely to sell, a subjective measure that would require survey data to substantiate. (Barnard and Butcher, 1981)

Another approach toward estimating developability, the Canadian Land and Infrastructure Mapping Program, operates in 27 of Canada's largest urban regions. (Spurr, 1980) It classifies residentially developable land as vacant land from the following categories:

- infrastructure serviced
- residentially zoned
- proposed for subdivision
- approved, but not built, subdivision
- owned by development firms, builders, or speculators
- with physical potential for development and located near above categories or in an area with development potential.

Available land supply is divided into time periods (available within one year, two-three years, four-five years, six or more years), depending on the degree to which it possesses certain vital characteristics. For example, the current land supply includes parcels with infrastructure, good drainage, and an approved subdivision. To test the land supply adequacy by time period, it is compared with a temporal projection of demand derived from demographic analyses for the same time periods.

D. Land Supply Information Issues

Monitoring and coordinating all the information desired by different users of land supply data is a complex task. To meet the full range of public and private user needs would require an interconnected land supply mega-system able to acquire and analyze land information from a variety of compatible government and market sources. Because the land information interests of government and private development groups intersect but are not exactly the same, and because of the changing status of the field of land information automation, experts do not agree on all important issues. The following issues, drawn from our case studies, telephone reconnaissance, and literature survey, describe major questions faced by existing systems.

What Information Do We Monitor? Most experts agree that land supply information systems should be organized on the basis of the land parcel, with provision for aggregating parcels into geographic subareas, such as planning districts or Census Tracts. They also agree that information is needed about vacant or underutilized land, zoning and other development regulations, planned use, assessments, and the timing and nature of public service availability. Beyond that, there is debate over whether market data, such as land price and availability for development, should be included in government systems or provided by compatible private systems. There also is debate about the feasibility of including information on environmental characteristics, such as slope and soils, since this is typically maintained in different form than parcel data and requires an overlay mapping capability to combine with parcel data.

How Broad Is the Public Sector's Responsibility to Provide Land Supply Information? The emergence of private land information services illustrates the possibility of dividing the responsibility for information provision. Government roles now range from "full service" systems that include the functions of comprehensive database generator, manager, and supplier, down to "basic" systems with limited functions of selected data generation and management and wholesaling of data to private suppliers who retail it to individual users. Many private services have carved out niches in the land information field, not only providing real estate data but also reducing the burden on governments to deal with the needs of individual customers for data from public files. These private services are built on government databases. However, if two organizations must enter the same data, as is the case where computer-to-computer transfer between public and private sectors is not provided for, the cost of information rises. The issue goes to the degree of responsibility assumed by government to meet information access needs of the private sector.

What Legal Pitfalls Underlie Land Information Provision? Part of the caution of governments in undertaking land information systems stems from potential legal pitfalls. Among legal issues are liability for supplying inaccurate information, inadequate definition of regulated areas, not protecting confidentiality, and failing to ensure access to public records. (Epstein and Chatterton, 1984) A Wisconsin Supreme Court case found that a land owner was entitled to compensation for loss due to misrepresentation on a government map of the high water mark around a lake where she owned land, which was claimed to put her ownership into question. (Zinn v State, 112 Wis. 2d 417, 334 N.W. 2d 67 (1983)) Tax assessors in our case study areas were reluctant to enter data from their field notes (beyond land use and condition) into computerized land information systems because of concern over potential inaccuracies if these data were to be used for other purposes.

What Form Does Data File Access Take? Access to land databases is provided through a variety of channels, ranging from reports published monthly, quarterly or annually, to custom printouts assembled on demand, to instantaneous online access from remote terminals. Periodic published reports have the advantages of data comparability and established trend series, as well as low public service demands. Custom reports provide timely data in the format desired by the user but require higher "information counter" staffing. Online access allows users to create their own reports but raises issues of file security and updating. In most government information systems, government agencies enjoy higher levels of accessibility than private users.

What Are the Problems of File Security? Two types of security problems arise with land information systems. First, the system must safeguard against unauthorized entry or manipulation of data. Because the public records in these systems are relied upon for critical public decisions ranging from tax assessment to rezoning, their integrity is a paramount concern. Second, the system must safeguard against unauthorized disclosure of private information. Governments are charged with maintaining the confidentiality of some data, such as police files and information about the financial affairs of individuals and businesses, and must ensure that it is not released to the public through access to a public information system. The system also should protect citizens from abuses of public information, such as the use of address files for marketing or political purposes. Many states have public records acts, such as the California Public Records Act of 1968, governing automated data files maintained by local governments.

How Often Are Files Updated? Ideally, all files are updated continuously, but this requires extensive staff and management effort to input and check data daily. In the case study jurisdictions, updating ranges from daily to weekly, monthly, quarterly, and even annually, depending on the type of data and the organization of the government information system. For example, continuously updated data usually includes building permits and land sales, while zoning changes are updated weekly or monthly and overall land supply tabulations are reported quarterly or annually. Within a single jurisdiction, updating of different data fields within a file varies according to the rate of change of the data and the use to which it is put. Since the currency of land supply information is critical for many market decisions, the tradeoff here is between the degree of data timeliness and the cost of conducting updates. This is related to the way that the information service is organized.

Is Entry of Land Information Centralized or Dispersed? Centralized data services, which assemble information from various sources into a central database, tend toward periodic rather than continuous data entry. When databases are distributed among a number of data collecting and maintaining organizations, data entry tends to be continuous. Often this difference is due to a difference in responsibility. The central data service is primarily an information library and re-

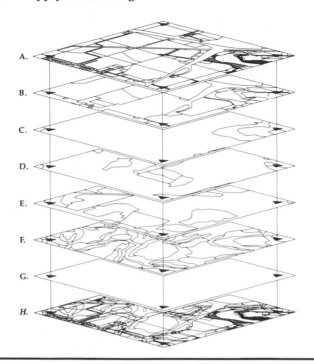

Section 22, T8N, R9E, Town of Westport, Dane County, Wisconsin

Data Layers:	Responsible Agency:
A. Parcels	Surveyor, Dane County Land Regulation and Records Department.
B. Zoning	Zoning Administrator, Dane County Land Regulation and Records Department.
C. Floodplains	Zoning Administrator, Dane County Land Regulation and Records Department.
D. Wetlands	Wisconsin Department of Natural Resources.
E. Land Cover	Dane County Land Conservation Committee.
F. Soils	United States Department of Agriculture, Soil Conservation Service.
G. Reference Framework	Public Land Survey System corners with geodetic coordinates.
H. *Composite Overlay*	*Layers integrated as needed, example shows parcels, soils and reference framework.*

Figure 2. *Concept for a multipurpose land information system. (Source: B. J. Niemann, Jr., and N. R. Chrisman,* Wisconsin Land Information Newsletter *2, No. 2, 1984.)*

porting agency, while the data collection organization is primarily an operating agency which uses its data in its daily operation. Most jurisdictions studied distribute data entry among operating departments. Even when centralized data processing is done, interactive software can allow continuous data entry by user departments. The issue of information service organization is one of the critical design choices a local government faces.

How Is Compatibility of Related Databases Ensured? In theory, data on land supply is compatible not only across governmental agencies, such as tax assessment and planning and public works, but also between the government and private organizations, such as realtors and development consultants, and across jurisdictions within the same metropolitan area, housing market, or planning region. There are three levels of concern here: 1) hardware compatibility, 2) software and file compatibility, and 3) geographic identifier compatibility. At minimum, a degree of intra-jurisdictional compatibility is achieved by using the same parcel identifiers (tax number, property address, and x-y coordinates), along with the same geographic subareas (planning districts, Census Tracts). Because assessment procedures, databases, and information systems differ among jurisdictions, it is much more difficult to ensure inter-jurisdictional compatibility.

What Types of Software Are Used? No longer do local governments have to design their own computer programs. Standard software is commercially available to manage databases, do spreadsheet analyses, generate reports, and produce graphics. Basic land information systems rely on verbal/numeric outputs. Advanced systems add mapping capabilities, either in the form of subarea characteristic patterns or digitized parcel maps. The most sophisticated systems allow different databases to be overlayed to form composite maps. (See Figure 2.) Modular system design permits capability expansion from basic to advanced over time, through progressive acquisition of equipment and software programs.

How Do Governments Initiate Land Supply Information Systems? System initiation is a gradual process, involving extensive coordination of information providers and users at the start, along with careful analysis of tasks and products. Sometimes a demonstration or pilot project is undertaken within a limited subarea to illustrate the usefulness, feasibility, and desirability of creating a system. Sometimes a small public/private joint venture is undertaken to test possibilities for cooperative data sharing. Initiators study both the data market and the data politics in their jurisdictions. The market for information is much "hotter" in an active development market, when accurate and timely land supply information can make or break both public growth policies and private development proposals. The politics of data provision revolve around questions of "turf", especially when information generators are perceived to curtail sharing of data access or resources.

III

Designing an Automated Land Supply Information System

There seems to be a substantial need for a more complete exchange of information about system design and applications.

John Hysom and Stephen Ruth
"A Nationwide Assessment of Local Government Planning Information Systems"

This chapter presents recommendations for designing an automated land supply information system, based on the findings of this study. After an overview of major system components, the following sections discuss data organization, system structure, hardware and software considerations, operating guidelines, land supply evaluation, and users and uses of land supply data. Recommendations are highlighted in italics. Readers desiring definitions of computer terms may consult the Glossary.

A. Definition of a Prototype ALSIS

An Automated Land Supply Information System (ALSIS) is defined as a computerized database that:

- *is organized around the land parcel as its basic unit, with the capability of aggregating parcel data by subareas,*
- *contains information about the existing and forecasted land supply within a jurisdiction, market, or region,*
- *is accessible to public and private sector users in convenient formats, and*

- *is designed for monitoring changes in land supply inventory in order to assist in management and regulation of land development, and to facilitate analysis of land markets.*

Public land supply information systems are clearly needed to monitor changes in vacant land in growing urban areas. They are invaluable in "hot" development markets, such as suburban high tech corridors, especially where growth management programs have been established. However, they are also useful in stable urban areas to facilitate sound land use planning, infill development, and capital improvement programming. As defined here, our prototype land supply information system is a basic tool for improving public policy information and market decision making in a variety of settings.

This prototype system can be viewed as an expanded or enhanced version of a conventional land use information system. An ALSIS differs from a conventional system in its increased attention to, and detail on, the supply side of the land use equation. It is more sensitive to pending changes in the supply of developable land due to projects under review, infrastructure changes, and policy constraints. It is more market-oriented. It goes beyond reporting of existing land use to tracking land supply dynamics. It is more of a long-range planning tool, taking into account future supply and demand needs.

Our recommendations on ALSIS design and implementation do not always distinguish between an ALSIS and a conventional land use information system. In practice, we found that system managers often saw land supply data provision simply as one more job for a land use information system. But we also found that many localities do not yet have even conventional systems in place. So our recommendations are geared toward those localities seeking complete new systems (land use information systems with ALSIS components), but they should also be useful to localities that only want to add an ALSIS component to an existing land use information system.

B. Data Organization

Contemporary land information systems should be organized around land parcels as their basic units. Thus, the ALSIS must be parcel based, and able to handle polygons which can describe irregular land ownership parcel shapes and boundaries. Also, it should be able to aggregate parcel data by various subareas, from subdivisions and projects, to Census Tracts and Blocks, planning districts, electoral districts, public facilities districts, and the like. If possible, the ALSIS database should be compatible with those of adjacent jurisdictions and private sector systems to facilitate metropolitan area, market area, and regional analyses. The system should not be organized around rectangular grids, as some early systems were, since grids do not reflect land ownership at the individual parcel level.

The ALSIS should cover both existing and forecasted land supply information, so that users can understand current and future supply situations. The existing land supply can be identified as vacant land that is zoned for development, has the necessary public services available, is not limited by physical constraints, such as floodplains or hazard areas, and is available for development. The forecasted land supply can be identified as vacant land that is planned for urban development, scheduled for public services, not limited by physical constraints, and will be available for development.

Accessibility to public and private users is enhanced by clear and logical data structures. Structurally, the two major types of ALSIS files are (see Figure 3):

1. The "parcel" file, derived from the assessor's records, and containing ownership, assessment, and land use data on each individual land parcel in the jurisdiction, and
2. the "project" file, derived from applications for subdivision plat, planned unit development, and site plan approval, and containing data on each proposed project and its stage in the process of development review (the pipeline).

In addition to the parcel and project files, separate files may be kept for other purposes, such as tracking building permits, sewer permits, and environmental conditions (soils, slope, floodplains). Each unit should update its own file.

"Identifiers" are unique parcel features that allow the system to locate and manipulate thousands of individual parcel records. Standard identifiers are the Assessor's Tax Number, the Parcel Address, and the X-Y map coordinates of the parcel or its centroid. By using any one of these identifiers, a user can call up information on particular parcels from various files.

Users should be able to enter the files through a series of "screens", which provide data formats organized around standard types of inquiries, such as an assessment inquiry which would include land and improvement valuations or a planning inquiry which would include existing and planned land use, for example. Tailoring these data capture screens to the specific information needed by a particular department or type of user allows easier and more efficient ALSIS operation, since extraneous data are not displayed.

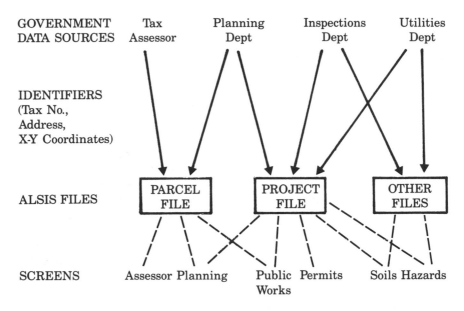

Figure 3. *Automated Land Information System components.*

A well organized system seeks to provide accurate and timely information in formats suitable for user needs. It is particularly important to ensure that private market-oriented information services are compatible with the ALSIS. Unless the public system undertakes to provide market information, such as land price and availability, it should cooperate with private services that do offer such information. Compatibility of hardware, software and files, and geographic identifiers should be a goal of system design. If all users seek to enter additional information to benefit the system, then a comprehensive database can be built.

The Parcel File

A parcel file should be created which combines an extract of the assessor's records with planning-related information entered by the Planning Department. Compatibility of ALSIS with computerized Multiple Listing Service (MLS) files should be encouraged. Parcel identifiers should include assessor's parcel number, address, and X-Y coordinates. The goal of the system should be that all parcels within the jurisdiction are included in the database. Land use codes should have "vacant" and "underutilized" classifications. The ability of a government to monitor the amount of vacant land having development potential (as defined by public policies) and available for development will provide the government with good supply estimates to relate to projected demand and to policy choices. Spatial disaggregation of the database into land and housing subareas will assist in the documentation of any differential effect of land use controls across space.

The first file to be compiled should be the Parcel File, with its database constructed so that the basic unit of tabulation is the tax parcel, as defined by the assessor. This level of specificity will increase the value of the database as a tool for both public policy and private development. The system should be able to aggregate parcel-based data to larger levels of geography (such as Census Tract or planning area).

The parcel file database should include selected information from the assessor's files as an initial basic building block. Along with the assessment records, planning-related data should be entered into the ALSIS database by the Planning Department. Data compiled on each parcel should include, when appropriate to the jurisdiction:

Valuation/Assessor's Data
Parcel identification number
Land use code (including "vacant" and "underutilized")
Acreage
Owner's name
Assessed value (land and improvement)
Tax status and legal description
Recent sales date and price

Regulations and Plans
Zoning classification
General Plan designation (land use, development category)
Density: presently allowed and planned
Infrastructure availability (water, sewer, roads)

Geographic Identifiers
Site address
Census tract (providing potential link to socioeconomic data of the
    Bureau of the Census)
Supervisorial or councilmanic district
Planning area
Special districts serving the parcel

Other geo-codes appropriate to the jurisdiction (sewershed, traffic zone, etc.)

Land Characteristics
Topography and slopes
Soils and septic potential
Watershed and aquifer recharge
Proximity to road (or road frontage)

Parcel History
"To-From" indicator, showing "parent" parcel numbers for newly created parcels or subdivision lots, and "child" parcel numbers for parcels which no longer exist.
Listing of major public actions requested and/or taken on the parcel

Compatibility of ALSIS with computerized Multiple Listing Service (MLS) files should be encouraged. The two sources of automated information should be compatible in terms of hardware, software and file structure, and geographic identifiers. This will increase the relevance of system information to private sector users. The combination of government and market data will create a unique and useful source of information to varied users. Merging of the two databases can occur via the property address identifier. This linking of ALSIS and MLS will provide private sector users of ALSIS with an indication of market availability of a particular parcel. Although not essential, the inclusion of assessor's data such as age of structure, construction type, and number of bathrooms in the ALSIS database will greatly facilitate housing market analyses.

Parcel identifiers should include assessor's parcel number, address (if any), and X-Y coordinates (when mapping capability is included). Address identification will enable the system to be linked to many outside sources (such as a MLS database). The user should be able to access particular parcels in the database by using any of these three identifiers. In addition, access by owner's name may also be desirable. Standardized address formats should be worked out before implementation of the system. Unique addresses must be developed, modifying assessor's address when necessary so that parcels can be accessed by unique street address.

The goal of the system should be complete data for all parcels in the jurisdiction and, in the case of cities, in the effective planning area. It may be more economically practical to enter a full set of data for a subarea at first, but the eventual system should include a jurisdiction-wide database. While the level of detail will vary across jurisdictions, the system should apply to the widest geographic area involved with local government decisions, often a county.

Land use codes will usually be entered into the system by the assessor's office. It is important to have a standardized listing of land use codes and definitions so that ambiguities are lessened in the future. It is also essential that there be set guidelines and criteria for assigning a particular land use code to a parcel. A jurisdiction should avoid assigning a "mixed use" code to those parcels where there is more than one land use because this practice will decrease the specificity and usefulness of the land use data. Techniques for dealing with mixed uses include: 1) coding only the predominant use (that usage covering the greatest portion of the lot, or the improvement with the highest assessed value), 2) coding the highest and best use, 3) devising a coding system that permits secondary uses to be coded, and 4) using building use codes as well as land use codes.

It will help the interpretation of land use codes if the first of the two digits refers to a general land use (residential, commercial, industrial, vacant), while the second digit more clearly defines the type of land use within a general category (single-family residential, apartment, duplex, condominium, etc.). It may also be beneficial to designate a temporary use code by following the code with a "99." It is essential that one of the land use codes be a "vacant" classification. In addition, it may be useful to have an "underutilized" classification, which will identify those parcels where the current density is significantly less that the potential density as determined by the zoning or General Plan designation. If classified as "underutilized", the current use of the parcel should be noted in a secondary field.

A "developable" or "buildable" definition for vacant land parcels is often subjective, time-dependent, and difficult for a government to determine. Nevertheless, governments which do not attempt to monitor the amount of vacant land having development potential which is actually available for development will not have good supply estimates to relate to projected demand and to policy choices. The public sector should not simply note that a given parcel is vacant with certain characteristics (zoning, physical limits, infrastructure availability), and assume that the user of ALSIS information will determine whether the vacant parcel is "developable" using his own criteria. The reluctance of many current systems to estimate "available" or "developable" land supply calls into question the validity of growth control policies based on an incomplete knowledge base. Methods and techniques for evaluating the adequacy of an existing land supply are examined in section III.F.

Residential subareas incorporated into ALSIS for analytical purposes should permit a logical and meaningful aggregation of relevant land use criteria by statistical area. Land use controls do not necessarily act uniformly over a region. The excess demand created by excessive controls in one submarket can shift to other submarkets as consumers search out substitute housing. Spatially disaggregating the database into land and housing submarkets will assist in determining the extent of this substitution effect. The methods for defining subareas vary from the simple (Census Tracts) to the complex (multivariate analysis). Dowall (1981) states that data availability should be given primary consideration when developing submarkets, and favors the Census Tract. Disaggregation into planning areas will increase the usefulness of the system for planners. Subareas can also be defined on the basis of multivariate analytical techniques (such as cluster or factor analysis), or through the use of household movement data. Having several sets of subareas, each defined by different criteria, will increase the relevance of the system's data to its varied users.

The Project File

A project file should be created to track projects and the public actions (such as rezonings, subdivisions, building permits, special permits) taken on those projects. Planning applications and building permit data should be stored on a single database mutually accessible to both planners and building inspectors. A permit should go through a stepped process of recording, with each step's completion signified by appropriate personnel "initialling" the screen.

The second file to be completed should be the Project File, which will track projects and public actions taken on those projects. The project file can be linked to the parcel file by assessor's parcel number or X-Y coordinates (when mapping capability is included). The project file can provide information important for current and mid-range planning purposes. In addition, by tracking development in the pipeline land out of the market due to current development can be subtracted from the vacant land supply. This will decrease the tendency of the system to overestimate available land supply.

Project data should include geographic identifiers so that information can be aggregated to a geographic area level. This will provide information on the degree of development activity occurring in a particular area, and will facilitate forecasting. Such "pipeline" (ongoing/ development activity can be added to existing development and compared to "build-out" figures based on the maximum development possible under the General Plan. Tracking of development activity by subarea also can be beneficial to private sector users. Examining, the "approved/considered" ratio for subdivision, rezoning, and special permit applications in a specific subarea will give the prospective builder a rough indication of the likelihood that his application will be approved. An additional important benefit of computerizing the development review process may be shortened project or proposal review times and better access to project review information for the private sector.

A permit tracking module should monitor a project from initial application to completion. It should track development projects through issuance of certificates of occupancy, rather than stopping at issuance of building permits. Building permits should be matched with final inspections data to indicate which construction projects were actually completed. This will enable planners and policy makers to judge actual versus estimated impacts on public facilities.

The permit tracking system should store data from planning applications and building permits on a single database mutually accessible to both planning and building inspection personnel. This will eliminate the duplicate entry of the same data and will improve the accuracy of data used for both purposes. A user should be able to gain access to a particular project file by either entering the owner's name or project application number.

A permit should go through a stepped entry process from initial planning application data to final building inspection project characteristics. For each step, the following information should be collected:

Type of permit
Action to be taken
Date scheduled
Date action taken
Action taken ("status")

When each step is complete, the responsible staff person "initials" the screen by appropriate password, signifying the completion of the particular step. The final permit should not be processed until all appropriate screens are initialled by approved personnel. The tracking module should also include an area for comments by appropriate public agencies reviewing the proposal. These comments become part of the history of the parcel record, and can be used for future reference in subsequent public actions concerning the parcel.

C. System Structure

Major questions on the organization of an automated land supply information system concern the distribution of computer equipment and responsibilities.

Organizational Options for Data Processing

It is recommended that a distributed form of data processing be used for the ALSIS if it is economically feasible. An alternative to the distributed form is the centralized form. If the data processing function is centralized, it is essential that data capture screens be tailored to user departments' needs. A good relationship between the data processing department and user departments must be maintained for the ALSIS to run smoothly.

Three structural or organizational options may be used for setting up a computerized land records system: 1) centralized, 2) decentralized, and 3) distributed (see Figure 4). A jurisdiction implementing an ALSIS should be aware of these structural alternatives, and the advantages and disadvantages of each:

- *Centralized*: computer facility (frequently a mainframe computer) is in one location, with a data processing department responsible for operation and maintenance. All user departments are tied to this one computer and its programs.
- *Decentralized*: minicomputer or microcomputer in individual user departments, each with own database relevant to the needs of that department. No use of a central mainframe as a data storage library.
- *Distributed*: Combines a central computer facility acting as a data library, and the ability of user departments to download subsets of the full database to computers housed in their departments. One possibility is a microcomputer for each functional area or department (planning, building inspection, public works, etc.) with a mainframe computer used as a centralized data library and housed in a data processing department. Micro-mini and mini-mainframe linkages are other examples of the distributed form of data processing. Some definitions of "distributed" data processing include all forms of remote-access systems. In this report, we

CENTRALIZED PROCESSING
(Terminals provide remote access for user
departments but not remote processing)

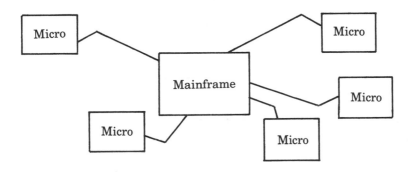

DISTRIBUTED PROCESSING
(Micro- or minicomputers provide both remote access
for user departments *and* remote processing through downloading)

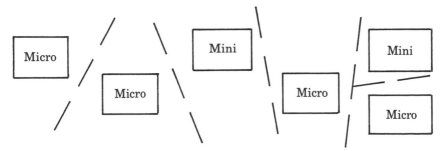

DECENTRALIZED PROCESSING
(Each user department has its own processing unit
and there is no central coordination between the
various units to guard against duplication)

Figure 4. *Structural options for ALSIS.*

define "distributed" systems more inclusively to be those where both access and processing is distributed.

Centralized systems concentrate computer resources and technical personnel in one department (data processing) and can lead to economies of effort and standardization of programs. They also can make user departments dependent on the data processing department, which is often involved in large, batch-mode computer runs on fixed time schedules. This can result in time delays in response to user departments' requests and questions. Centralized systems are also vulnerable to having the whole system knocked out by a power surge.

Decentralized systems provide the opportunity to have databases customized to the needs of the user departments, and increase the reliability of the system. A power surge or controller error will probably not knock out the whole system because of multiple databases in different locations. However, decentralized systems provide no linkage between the different databases and are susceptible to duplication of effort across departments.

Distributed systems combine features of both centralized and decentralized structural forms. Customized databases available for user departments are linked together by a data library mainframe or minicomputer which contains the full database. There still might be a tendency for some duplication of effort across departments, but it will be less than in the decentralized form. User department dependence on the data processing department will be lessened, giving more analytical autonomy to the user departments.

A jurisdiction implementing an ALSIS should strongly consider a distributed system because of its superior ability to meet the needs of the user departments by providing analytical autonomy from the data processing department. The most important consideration to keep in mind is that the data needs of the various user departments must be met. If this does not happen, user department dissatisfaction with the system will often lead to an incomplete and out-of-date database.

A distributed, mainframe-micro (or minicomputer-microcomputer) linked system gives a user department the ability to create database subsets customized to the particular department. Government can still take advantage of the central mainframe's or minicomputer's capability to store a lot of data and handle a lot of communication. The central computer library can act as a coordinative force, holding together the numerous computers and databases resident in the various user departments. At the same time, there is the distribution (through downloading) of the real processing power to the personal computer, which is more comfortable and easy to use. In addition, the cost of buying a set of microcomputers can often be justified on the basis of word processing alone.

If a jurisdiction does not find this distributed structure appropriate for its needs, or finds that it is not economically feasible, another alternative is to have a centralized form with data capture screens customized for individual departments. If a centralized form is to be used, it is essential that interactive software be used which orients updating, modification, and retrieval procedures to the needs of the user department. The parcel file, for instance, can have a "planning inquiry" which lists pertinent planning-related items such as zoning, planning area, acreage, and so on. An "assessor inquiry" could be designed which would list parcel-specific data elements such as tax, valuation, and legal description. Updating and retrieval would both be possible by accessing the "inquiry" related to the information to be updated or retrieved. The database, segmented into different inquiries to fit the needs of the several user departments, would still be held together by the various parcel identifiers common to all inquiries (parcel number, address, X-Y coordinates, owner). In addition, a "general data inquiry" could combine and summarize the most commonly accessed information from each of the separate inquiries. Menu-driven programs would be necessary, providing the user with a choice between the different types of inquiries. Other common types of "inquiries" (tailored data capture screens) possible include: building inspection, owner, situs, permits-applications, and Census Tracts. The type of data capture screens available should be consistent with the needs of the user departments which are doing the updating and retrieval.

If the centralized form of data processing is used, a crucial issue will be the relationship between the department operating and maintaining the mainframe and its programs (the "host") and the various user departments. A centralized data processing form can potentially lead to conflicts over authority, resources, and the placement of the mainframe function. In the jurisdictions studied, the mainframe computer was often the responsibility of the data processing department and, less frequently, a research/statistics department. Other possible locations for mainframe responsibility include the assessor's office, the city manager/county administrator's office, or the planning department.

Huxhold (1980) examined five inter-departmental factors which can impede effective computer use: differing goals, different modes of operation, unrealistic expectations from the "host" and user departments, lack of communication, and organizational restrictions. The problem of differing modes of operation between the planning and the host data processing departments was apparent in the Contra Costa County and San Diego case studies. Much of the work of the planning departments was ad hoc, one-time analyses, politically driven, and with timely results taking priority over cost and efficiency. The data processing department, on the other hand, was concerned with the efficient design of the computer system and with programs designed to run repetitively on a daily or annual basis.

Several organizational/personnel options are available and should be considered during the design phase of the ALSIS. These options are:

a. designation of a person within each user department who can represent the department's interests (generally should be someone in an administrative position, not a technician).
b. programmer/analyst actually working within each of the user departments; "decentralization of technicians."
c. specified liaison within the host department able to answer inquiries from user departments.
d. ALSIS staff separate from both user departments and host department; staff acting as medium or funnel, able to speak both the technical language of the host department and the practical language of user departments.

The effectiveness of an organizational option will be largely dependent on the inter-departmental atmosphere existing prior to the implementation of the ALSIS. Experience from the case studies shows the presence of varied approaches. Fairfax and Montgomery Counties have specified liaisons within the host departments (in both cases, a research and statistics office). Lane County and the City of San Diego designate a person within each of the user departments to represent the department's interests. In fact, San Diego has positioned the system coordinator within the planning department. San Diego's earlier attempt to have a system administrator separate from both host and user departments has not succeeded. Contra Costa County is satisfied with its ALSIS staff separate from both host and user departments. New Haven's system, due to its microcomputer emphasis, allows almost complete autonomy for the user department. It should be stressed that one of the strong advantages of a distributed form of data processing is that it provides for database and analytical autonomy for user departments and thus tends to avoid potential organizational conflict over ALSIS authority and resources.

D. Hardware and Software Considerations

We simply cannot track land supply and update frequently without computerization.

> Bob Johnson
> Research Section, Planning
> Department
> City of Phoenix

Critical design decisions will involve what types of hardware and software should be acquired and when. System development will often evolve over time and should be visualized as a modular process. Computer mapping capability should be planned for in the design phase, and should be incorporated into the system when economically feasible.

Hardware Considerations

Recent computer technology has muddied the dividing lines between types of hardware. It is useful to think in terms of the jobs that computer hardware should do, including data storage, database management, database access, data analysis, report generation, graphics and mapping, and the like. Excess hardware capacity should be acquired initially so that the system can expand in the future without encountering storage constraints.

The question of whether to select a mainframe computer, a minicomputer, or a microcomputer, or some combination of these, for an automated land supply information system is not an easy one to answer and will often depend on three factors:

- the type of computer technology which currently exists within government.
- the organizational framework (centralized versus distributed) desired by the monitoring government.
- the software capabilities needed or desired by the monitoring jurisdiction.

A useful way to address the hardware question is in terms of the abilities of the hardware, the characteristics of local information needs, and the work to be done. There are two main considerations in deciding on hardware: 1) memory/storage and 2) processing time. Instead of suggesting a particular hardware-software combination, this section will explore several options available in today's market.

Mainframe computers are the traditional medium and large-scale computer systems used in most organizations for 1) information processing in a centralized or distributed mode, and 2) data communications applications where terminals at remote locations transmit data to a central processing unit.

Minicomputers are rapidly increasing in popularity, especially when the computer system is decentralized among several departments. Minis are ideal for a decentralized computer system because they are small, yet powerful enough for many applications. In addition, minis can be useful for distributed functions, taking some of the load off the mainframe computer. Cost gives the minicomputer an advantage over the mainframe, while memory size is beginning to overlap between the two types of computer hardware.

The popularity of microcomputers has been revolutionary. In addition to word processing, micros have been used as terminals that can access an organization-wide database or can transmit messages, and as professional workstations for managers to perform calculations, answer inquiries, and analyze data. The microcomputer is often excellent as a module in a distributed computer system because the user can download subsets of the full database onto the micro, and have a database customized to the user's needs.

If the database is large (many parcels, with multiple records per parcel), the system may require large data storage capacity, such as that of a mainframe or minicomputer. A minicomputer can be an attractive possibility because of cost, storage, and speed considerations and user friendliness. Mainframe or minicomputers can be linked to microcomputers, providing users with the ability to download relevant subsets to the micro. Minicomputers are often easier to use than mainframes, and they also can separate the database from the sometimes inflexible or slow procedures of a central data processing department. In addition, minis are able to handle large data sets (between 400 and 600 megabytes). Another consideration is that the current hardware and software environment for interactive computer mapping is primarily a minicomputer one. This is due, in part, to the fact that the intensive mathematical computational power needed for geographic processing has been available on minicomputer systems. Montgomery County (MD), Houston, and San Jose currently use minicomputers to house their databases. Montgomery County uses a Hewlett Packard

3000 minicomputer to house the full database, a Hewlett Packard 9000 super microcomputer for graphics and modeling, and ten Hewlett Packard 150 microcomputers used as terminals.

Even with large databases, it should be kept in mind that microcomputers can be used to sort, manipulate, and analyze *subsets* of the total ALSIS database. For such "downloading" from the mainframe to the micro to occur, the user must know the parameters of the desired subset. Often, "link software" can be purchased which translates mainframe data formats directly into popular microcomputer file formats. The advantages of microcomputer use include: customized data sets for individual users and user departments, speed of operations, less costly computer runs, freedom from constraints of multi-user mainframe systems, and good editing capabilities. Contra Costa County (CA) is currently using microcomputers in the planning department to download subsets of the full mainframe-housed database onto the micro. The planning department uses an IBM PC-XT with a 10 megabyte hard disk. Sorting of the full database is too big an operation for the XT and interactive mainframe software is required. However, sorting of a subset with pre-specified parameters can be done with the XT using vendor micro software.

Often, a stand-alone (micro or mini) monitoring system would be appropriate for smaller jurisdictions or where monitoring is focused on activities pertinent to a single government department. The Office of Housing and Neighborhood Development in New Haven uses a super microcomputer with 512K bytes of random access memory (RAM) and a forty megabyte hard disk drive. The data collection files, composed of approximately 46,500 records, occupy approximately 10 megabytes of the hard disk unit, while the resident software program modules require approximately 3 megabytes of storage. Processing and information retrieval times vary considerably, depending upon the information being sought. The single most influential factor regarding inquiry response time appears to be the presence or absence of a secondary index on the field(s) involved. The existence of such a secondary index can reduce an inquiry involving the parcel file from fifteen minutes to three seconds. The entire parcel file (26,000 records at 360 bytes per record) can be completely searched in about fifteen minutes. The most common inquiries have proven to be the simple ones which use secondary indices, and provide a response time in seconds. (New Haven Office of Housing and Neighborhood Development, 1984). Sacramento (CA) is another example of a microcomputer-based system. Its vacant land survey update was done on an IBM-PC with hard disk.

Cities or counties with growth management policies would need a system more fully integrated with public works, building inspections, and financial analysis data. Such as inter-departmental database may require the larger storage capacity of a late-model mainframe or minicomputer. The City of San Diego, for example, has found it necessary to have a centralized mainframe (IBM 3031) system because of the sheer size of the database (approximately one-third million records).

Software Considerations

Software capability needs will likely grow over time as system use becomes more varied. Recommended software capability is based on an interactive, on-line system in order to increase data currency and facilitate data analysis and queries. The choice between micro-based software and mainframe-based interactive software will be based on the form of data processing chosen (distributed or centralized). Vendor-produced software is often very effective and should be strongly considered. In-house programs should be relied on only to fill the gaps in the vendor-produced software. A hierarchical database structure will improve accessing ability, and a relational structure will increase sorting capability.

Software capability needs for the automated land supply information system include:

- Database manager: for file maintenance, updates, and report generation.
- Spreadsheet: for data analysis and "what-if" queries.
- Overlay: for aggregating parcel or area characteristics.
- Statistical: for correlation, trend, and forecasting analyses.
- Graphics display: for generating plotted business type charts and graphs, such as bar and XY plots.
- Computer mapping: for digitization of parcel boundaries for map analysis and presentations.
- Network analysis: for transportation and utility-related system analyses.

Software capability needs will likely expand over time as the system matures. A basic system should include a database manager (for basic editing and updating) and software for sorting and aggregation of data. A more advanced system would add spreadsheet, statistical, and graphics capabilities. Computer mapping and network analysis would usually come last due to cost considerations.

The system should be designed for interactive, on-line operation.

This increases the currency of the database, and allows responses to user-initiated inquiries to show up on the terminal within a short time, thus facilitating analysis. Changing a currently batch-oriented assessor record system to on-line will mean that current types of updates (ownership changes, new parcels) will occur immediately and outputs relative to these updates may be produced immediately. This will greatly facilitate the obtaining of accurate, current information for the public and government users. The importance of up-to-date information for private sector users of the system (such as market analysts) means that an on-line ALSIS, as opposed to batch-oriented, will increase the attractiveness of the monitoring system for private sector users. In addition, software procedures should be menu-driven, providing the user with a list of available machine functions for selection by the operator. Menu-driven software is especially beneficial to those users unfamiliar with the database contents or with computer operations generally.

Software and hardware should be chosen in the design stage which will allow refinements to the system to be incorporated later. The selection of software packages should be done at the same time as the selection of hardware. Indeed, in many cases, the software capabilities needed by the jurisdiction will drive the choice of hardware.

A choice which might have to be made is between micro-based software and mainframe-based interactive software for individual user needs. The advantages of mainframe-based interactive software include: single users can get at mainframe databases, common software for all users means higher efficiency on training and support, and transferability of data and routines. The advantages of micro-based software include: a large and growing market of flexible, multipurpose software packages, and the ability to tailor a database subset to fit the unique needs of the user.

Examples of mainframe-based interactive software use include San Diego, Charlotte, and Fairfax County. The City of San Diego, in their centralized data processing atmosphere, uses in-house programs and SAS for analysis, graphics and reporting of data. In addition, a query language (ASI/INQUIRY) is used which allows direct access to the database. Such a query language eliminates the need to develop standard report programs for specialized use. Charlotte (NC) uses ADR DataComp DP database management software to access their mainframe-housed database. Fairfax County uses EASYTRIEVE to access the database housed in the IBM 3083 mainframe.

The main types of micro-based software used in information systems are predominantly database managers and electronic spreadsheets.

Database managers are software packages designed to provide users with a fully integrated management information system. A database management system includes techniques for creating, updating, and querying files, as well as reporting on file information. Electronic spreadsheets are programming packages that enable people to make projections, test "what-if" hypotheses, and build models. They are useful for forecasting, financial analysis, inventory analysis, and budget preparation. Examples of micro-based software use include New Haven, Contra Costa County, and Denver. New Haven uses UNIFY database management software which includes a report writer feature, a user controlled help facility, a retrieval and update language, and data import and export capabilities. Contra Costa County uses R-base 5000 database manager along with Lotus 1-2-3 to retrieve and manipulate downloaded data from the full database housed in the IBM mainframe. Denver, in their mainframe-microcomputer distributed system, uses R-base 4000 and SPSS-PC to access and analyze data subsets.

Another software choice is between vendor-produced software and in-house programs. Vendor software (such as SAS and IDMS on the mainframe, and Lotus 1-2-3 and R-base 5000 on the micro) should be strongly considered when evaluating software alternatives. While vendor software still requires some programming for specific applications, it does not require the program design effort needed to create an in-house program. Some vendor-produced packages can almost be used exclusively in a system, from tailored data capture screens to management reports to what-if queries. San Diego has found that SAS provides users throughout the city with easy interactive tools for handling automated data. With the assistance of programmer/analysts, almost any data contained in files and databases maintained on city mainframe computers can be loaded into SAS for use by professional staff. Business chart and graph capabilities are provided as well as spreadsheet and statistical analysis tools.

Selection of a vendor-produced database software package that is popular and widely used will mean that the jurisdiction can more easily hire people with appropriate experience. Internally developed (in-house) computer programs, on the other hand, tend not to get updated regularly and often suffer from poor documentation which narrows the scope of potential users. Poor software documentation can be particularly harmful in an environment of multiple public and private sector users.

Two complementary methods of organizing the ALSIS database are the hierarchical and the relational structures. Choice of structure will affect the ability to access and sort parcel records.

A "hierarchical" database structure ("grandfather-fatherson") is set up so that access to information can be directed to either general data elements (common to all user departments) or to data fields more specific to a particular user department. For example, a "general data screen" would show data elements common to all inquiries, such as address, owner's name, and parcel number, in addition to listing other general data elements commonly accessed by various departments (land use code and acreage, for instance). A "planning inquiry screen", meanwhile, would contain data elements specific to the interests of the Planning Department, and would contain such items as zoning and General Plan designation, and land characteristic information. A hierarchical structure will lead to more efficient searches for parcel-specific information because information extraneous to the user's needs can be bypassed. Programs should be menu-driven whenever possible in order to facilitate use. Menu-driven programs present the user with a choice of options at selected decision points in the program.

A database which is "relational" in nature links common data elements within a database or across databases. This structure increases the ease with which sorts can be done. Links between data fields can be added or deleted in the future, thus increasing the flexibility of the monitoring system. "Chaining" can associate parcel records that have some element or attribute in common based on the record content and not the physical location of the record. A chain represents a logical path through a database by linking groups of records together for purposes of inquiry or updating. Several chains can be used for each parcel record so that numerous chains can be established, each for a different purpose. An example is where a user wishes to locate, or access, all parcels zoned R-20 in the parcel file. A relational database is set up so that each parcel record with R-20 zoning will be linked with all other parcel records having an R-20 zoning field.

Computer Mapping

Each jurisdiction implementing an ALSIS should plan to include computer mapping capability. While computer mapping may not be feasible initially, it may become possible later and the system should be designed to accommodate mapping. Three levels of mapping should be considered: 1) subarea characteristic maps, 2) parcel maps digitized from tax assessor's records or aerial photos, and 3) engineering quality maps of public infrastructure, such as sewer, water, and utility lines.

Mapping capability should become part of the ALSIS as soon as economically feasible, and should be incorporated into the design phase of the system. The computer generated map expands the visual communication of tabulated data and provides a spatial analysis of data that can only be observed or comprehended graphically. Spatial patterns are important in any analysis because they describe the distribution of an activity or incidence, and the patterns illustrated may point to trends in terms of directions, extent, and magnitude between two or more points in time.

Digital maps have evolved in recent years with the development of powerful data-processing systems that have made it possible to collect and store digitized map data. Manipulation and merging of the digitized data and selective retrieval of desired levels of land use data, either in graphic form as a plot or a printout or in numerical form as a body of data, can make the digitized representation of map information a very flexible form. With the development of the techniques of automated cartography, digital mapping promises to be the form most responsive to the requirements for flexible selection of type and amount of map information and for regular map updating.

The flexibility of being able to assemble a composite map of different levels of digital map data, and update and extract those levels in a timely manner as new information becomes available, is only possible with an interactive graphics system working with the map information in digital form. The interactive graphics system is the working tool for digital data storage and manipulation. Some of functions that can be performed by an interactive graphics system include: creation of a digital map database including numeric and graphic information on individual parcels or larger subareas, editing of the digital map database, and the producing of reports from various subsets of the database in tabular form.

Three levels of computer mapping should be considered: subarea characteristic maps capable of combining several overlays, parcel maps digitized from tax assessor's records or aerial photos, and engineering quality maps of public infrastructure networks. These three levels are presented here in the order of increasing specificity and required accuracy. The first two levels should definitely be part of ALSIS, with the inclusion of the third level dependent on cost considerations.

Boundaries of subareas (such as Census Tracts or planning areas) should be digitized initially so that socioeconomic information can be analyzed at these aggregative levels. Overlay capability (aggregation) and computer mapping capability should be linked in terms of entering hard copies of existing environmental resource overlays. It will often be more feasible to digitize environmental data on an overlay basis rather than on a parcel-specific basis. Physical data (such as topography, soils, septic potential, slope, watershed, and aquifer recharge) should be digitized before parcel boundaries because it will take less time and produce quicker results.

Parcel boundaries will be more time consuming than subarea boundaries, and also demand a higher level of accuracy. Parcel boundaries can be digitized from either existing assessor's parcel maps or from aerial photos. It is important that each property line segment have its own unique identifier and record that includes the identifiers of its end points as well as the parcels that it bounds. This will increase the ability to update the digital database as conditions change, and make it easier to test the digital database for completeness and consistency.

The mapping of public infrastructure lines and networks will require the highest level of accuracy. Such mapping will increase the relevance of ALSIS to public works departments and public utilities. Cooperation between the monitoring jurisdiction and a public utility company wishing to have computer mapping capabilities will result in a common map database surveyed to the highest level of accuracy. A common map database, accessible to both the monitoring jurisdiction and a public utility company, is a future possibility in three of the six case study jurisdictions.

The digitization of X-Y coordinates for parcel and infrastructure mapping should be to engineering standards. Such stringent standards means that care should be taken in assigning the digitizing tasks. Inaccurate or sloppy digitizing will greatly diminish the usefulness of the map database, and will also waste money. For this reason, it is not recommended that student interns be used for digitization. Instead, the monitoring jurisdiction should investigate the possibility of contracting out the tasks to a service bureau trained in the procedures. This will ensure quality control, while at the same time freeing full-time staff personnel from the time-consuming digitizing tasks. If staff personnel are used, a quality control mechanism should be in place to guard against inaccurate digitizing.

Another approach to computerized mapping of areas larger than the parcel (such as Census Tracts and Blocks) for localities is the U.S. Bureau of the Census GBF/DIME (Geographic Base File/ Dual Independent Map Encoding) system. Use of GBF/DIME would allow the parcel and permit files to be coded to census and political geography, and will be most useful in an ALSIS for mapping and analysis of subareas. Parcel digitization is not a standard part of the Census system so the use of DIME for parcel specific representation is limited. However, for Census Tracts and Blocks, DIME would provide access to data derived from the decennial Census of Population and Housing, an important source of information in a planning and analysis context. Many agancies are unable or unwilling to duplicate the work performed by the Census Bureau. For those jurisdictions wishing such information, the DIME system would provide a vital and necessary link between local geography and Census bureau information in an automated setting.

E. Operating Guidelines

Important operating matters include data entering and updating, reporting, access, and security.

Data Entering and Updating

Entering of information should be the responsibility of the user department most involved in the use of such information. Daily and weekly updates are recommended, with frequency of updating dependent on type of information and department. Reliability of data entry and modification should be assured.

Each agency or department should be responsible for its data's input, accuracy, and compatibility with the overall system. Still, a single system administrator should be responsible for coordinating the overall system. The system administrator's office would monitor the compatibility of input from different departments, review updates daily, and handle user-identified corrections.

Data should be updated daily for building permits and recorded instruments. Updates for zoning changes, new infrastructure, and other planning-related items should be at least weekly. Full-time staff should be assigned to updating tasks.

A quality control method should be designed so as to check the reliability of data entry. Entry "screens" should have identification on them regarding the data entry person. Departmental responsibility for editing data must be carefully decided on and tightly controlled. User corrections should be encouraged (but checked) so that database reliability improves with usage. It is important to remember that as system use increases, the more checks there are on the accuracy of the data.

Periodic Summary Reports

Development trends by geographic area should be detailed periodically based on information on "pipeline" development collected by the project file. Periodic summary reports are important because they provide easy access to system data for staff and the public, and because periodic hard-copy printouts will help provide a recorded history of development activity.

Summary reports should be produced at regular intervals showing development trends by geographic area. The source of this information is the project file. For each planning area, or other meaningful aggregative level (such as supervisorial or councilmanic district), existing plus ongoing ("pipeline") development should be compared to the build-out capacity of the area according to the General Plan. Such pipeline development includes subdivisions, rezonings, building permits, and special permits, and can be recorded so as to indicate whether the permit has been approved, or is under consideration. The time of future impact of pipeline development should be based on the type of permit and stage of that permit. For instance, time of future impact for residential units under construction could be forecast for 0-1 years in future; effect of final subdivision maps approved forecast for 1-3 years in future; and effect of rezonings approved forecast for 1-5 years in future. Graphic presentation of this material in the summary report, alongside raw figures, would make the report easier to understand.

Periodic summary reports are important for two main reasons. First, they provide both staff and the public with access to system data without the need to do extensive searches. Second, periodic printouts of summary data will provide insights into the development history and direction for the subarea. For more detailed information on appropriate report formats and uses of land supply data, refer to section III. G.

Access to ALSIS Information Within Government

We use the system to design housing programs, not just to provide information.

Gerardo Canto
Director, Office of Housing and
Neighborhood Development
City of New Haven

The bottom-line objective of the monitoring system is to assist the policy-making process.

George Orman
City Planning Department
San Diego, CA

Wide use by different government departments should be encouraged by maintaining a policy of "open access" to system information. City council or supervisorial staff should have online access to ALSIS information. User training and documentation will be very important to council or supervisorial staff. Thus, training meetings should be held by the system coordinator to teach staff about the system's technicalities, capabilities, and limitations. If the host jurisdiction is a county government, online access by member cities would be beneficial to all concerned.

System access should be available for wide use by different government departments. Extra data fields should be designed so that a user department can later add data elements needed by that department. User departments and city council or supervisorial staff should have the capability for on-line retrieval of system information. Council and supervisorial staff, in particular, need to be informed about the system's capabilities and limitations. Regular training meetings held by the system coordinator should emphasize that the system is a decision-*support* tool, not a decision-*making* tool. Potential misinterpretation of system data by council or supervisorial staff members should be guarded against by providing the appropriate user department with the chance to comment on data retrieved from the system.

If the implementing jurisdiction is a county government, online access by member cities is a possibility. Such access can be by modem or through dedicated lines. This possibility should be seriously considered because data accuracy will increase as the number of inputting governments increases (given clear operating guidelines, quality control, and adequate user training). Monthly user charges (and setup fees) should be set for member cities desiring on-line access. The cities would have access to the database as well as being capable of adding information on parcels within their city limits. In addition, a city entering building permit data would have such information electronically transmitted to the County Assessor.

Private Sector Access to ALSIS Information

We can't do without the information supplied by the computer information system. Without the system, the information is too spread out. We have a vast computerized record system within our company, but it contains information only on existing structures. We have a definite need for a database containing information on vacant land parcels.

> Joseph Mottola
> Merrill Lynch Commercial
> San Diego

Parcel-specific questions and small search requests should be answered by staff members at public counters. Larger search requests demand that another procedure be used. On-line private sector access is a possibility worth investigating because the commercial value of ALSIS information is promising. The eventual goal of ALSIS should be the ability of the private sector to download on at least a full cost basis. Cost of private sector online access should be on a per terminal (access point) per month basis, plus a one-time setup charge which covers user training.

Parcel or project-specific system information should be accessible at the Zoning Counter in the Planning Department or at a Development Assistance Counter in the Building Inspection Department. Staff should be available to do small searches, and answer questions about specific parcels or projects. Most uses of the system to answer private sector requests will deal with information on one or a few parcels. A hard copy list of parcels by address (e.g., "Main St., 125, owner Harry Hopkins) will facilitate the answering of parcel-specific questions by the public.

There should be a different procedure for private sector requests aimed at more time-intensive searches ("I'd like to know all parcels zoned R-20 with no slope constraints in planning area H"). These requests should be referred to designated personnel in either the user departments or Data Processing. A jurisdiction should have a set policy regarding private sector requests for tailored summary data that is not regularly reported in summary fashion. Several jurisdictions interviewed are wrestling with the following types of questions as private sector interest in system information increases. How much staff time are user departments willing to commit to doing computer runs tailored to fit the needs of a private sector request? How much should the jurisdiction charge? (Some state statutes require that all costs to the public for information be assessed on a cost-recovery basis only–meaning in this case computer time and report costs only). Does the jurisdiction want to assess a hourly research charge for such work to recover costs of computer and staff time? If a jurisdiction is limited to distributing information on a cost recovery basis only, is it feasible to spin off the monitoring system into a public, chartered, non-profit organization which is able to charge market rates for such information?

On-line private sector access to system information (retrieval only) is another possibility worth investigating. Again, modem access or dedicated lines could be used for private sector on-line access. The commercial value of such information for realtors, marketing analysts, title companies, appraisers, and developers is promising. Title companies, in particular, seem well suited for on-line access. The cost saving to title companies and real estate firms should easily pay the cost of searching and recording key elements from recorded documents. Review appraisals would become more exacting since the system would allow a simple check of the comparables used. The use of the information by market analysts and developers to document growth trends and find leads on developable parcels could be large. The eventual goal of ALSIS should be to provide the private sector with the ability to download subsets of the database.

If a jurisdiction is interested in private sector on-line access, it should market the system initially to private organizations such as Boards of Realtors, Chambers of Commerce, Homebuilders' Associations, and local non-profit Development Corporations. On-line access at these centralized locations is clearly economically practical for private sector users, and would tend to "spread the word" about the information system and its potential benefits to the private sector.

The costing of private sector on-line access should evolve over time from marginal cost to at least full cost. User charges and fees should be set for private sector on-line access. User charges should be per terminal (access point) per month. Also, there should be a one-time setup charge, which would include the training of the private sector participant on how to do on-line searches, and initial technical support. Initially, monthly user charges should be on a marginal cost basis in order to increase private sector use. Eventually, monthly user charges would be on at least a full cost recovery basis, which might include billing on time of use as well as number of access terminals.

User Training

Two types of training are needed for using an ALSIS: 1) systems operations, and 2) system applications. Applications workshops should be held along with technical operations workshops for all existing and potential users of the system. Users must be educated as to the capabilities of the system, and as to what questions can now be asked which were not possible before.

Operational training teaches the user how to log-on, search, and access system information. In itself, this technical training is not enough for the user to derive full benefit from the system. Applications training attempts to make the user aware of the kinds of questions which can now be asked which were not possible to answer before ALSIS. With increased computer technology comes a broader range of potential land information inquiries.

Both types of workshops should be held for all existing and potential users of the system. Both private sector and government individuals could participate in these workshops, and different workshops could be focused on the different information needs of particular groups of users. For instance, the homebuilders' association could hold a workshop on the new ways developers in the area have found for using ALSIS, and the benefits derived from such use. These workshops could be used as an arena for crossfertilization of ideas concerning ways to use the automated land supply information system for analyzing policy impacts, market trends, and development feasibility.

Security and Confidentiality

Three forms of security are available and recommended: 1) terminal, 2) password, and 3) update. Security considerations will become more important with increased and varied use of the system's information and should be a strong point of an ALSIS. The system should present no new problems of confidentiality because no new land information is being made public which was not already available.

System security should be such that some users/terminals may only retrieve and read system information, while other users/terminals can also update and modify information. Three types of security are available (terminal, password, and update), and all three should be used when access to system information is available to multiple public and private sector users. Terminal identification security will allow only certain terminals to retrieve ALSIS information and is used predominantly to control the number of access points. Password security ty allows only certain users to access system information. Update security, the most stringent of the three types, identifies which data elements can be updated or modified by whom (updater first has to be identified through terminal and password identification). Update security is aimed at protecting against unauthorized database modifications and sabotage.

If member cities are tied-in to a county host system, the cities should be restricted in their data entering and modifying to the range of parcel numbers found within their city limits. In cases of multiple-entering departments and governments, system security should be developed to the data field/element level (only certain users can modify certain data elements) if effective control is desired.

It is important that the jurisdiction implementing the system be aware of the potential problems over what information should and can be available to the public on an on-line basis. All states and the District of Columbia have public records laws based mainly on the Federal Freedom of Information Act (5 U.S.C. 552). FOIA is the chief federal open records law which provides that "any person" has the right, enforceable in court, to access to all federal "agency records," except those records that are covered by one of FOIA's exemptions. The wording of these exemptions has generated numerous disputes and uncertainties (Bouchard and Franklin, 1980/1982). Three important types of records which are exempted from the open records law are:

- internal agency matters which are more or less trivial in the sense that there is not a substantial and legitimate public interest in their disclosure.
- trade secrets and other confidential business information furnished to an agency outside the government.
- information about individuals, disclosure of which would be a "clearly unwarranted invasion of personal privacy". Information about an individual may invade privacy if it is information which he "could reasonably assert an option to withhold from the public at large because of its intimacy or its possible adverse effects upon himself or his family."

Most state public records laws are derived from the federal wording and often contain the same types of exemptions. The "public records" definitions incorporated into state statutes either explicitly cite "computer tapes and discs" as public records or implicitly include automated information by stating that public records are covered by the statute "regardless of physical form." In Connecticut, the statute states that "any public agency which maintains its records in a computer storage system shall provide a printout of any data properly identified" (Bouchard and Franklin, 1980/1982). Some jurisdictions have been able to modify public records statutes to shield their citizens. Santa Clara County (CA) releases only fundamental characteristics and aggregated information to the public (New Haven Office of Housing and Neighborhood Development, 1984). Other states, such as Connecticut, provide for broad access of information by the public.

Because of the variance and complexity of state public records laws, a jurisdiction wishing to initiate an ALSIS is strongly encouraged to contact its city or county counsel and state attorney-general regarding the possible effect of the relevant public records law on the distribution of ALSIS information.

Access to information about the financial affairs of individuals and business is often restricted because that type of information is viewed as being confidential and falling under one of the exemptions of state law. Most types of land information, however, are considered to be public information. Nevertheless, concern that computerization will make it easier to compile information about the land ownerships of particular individuals, or facilitate mass mailings, may raise some concern. In the fear that this type of information violates privacy, objections may be raised to implementation of ALSIS. System developers should remind those objectors that no new information is being made public that was not already available. It is, in actuality, interpretation of the system's data that can potentially lead to controversy, not the existence of ALSIS itself.

F. Evaluating Land Supply

We record vacant land as that which lacks improvements. We stay away from other definitions such as "developable" or "buildable" because they are too subjective.

> Lee Hemminger
> Senior Planner
> City of Stockton, CA.

We had trouble with the building industry at first because they thought we were soft on the definition of "buildable" and thus overestimated supply.

> Michael Munson
> Program Manager for Research
> Metro Council of Twin Cities

We have had definitional problems with our classification of land supply and have done qualitative studies to determine whether a parcel is really developable or not.

> Dennis Siglinger
> Data Services Division
> Denver Planning Office

An effective ALSIS will have a definition of available land supply which is mutually agreed upon by both government and private interests. Seven methods and techniques are recommended here which will give a truer picture of the amount of vacant land actually available, and will measure the adequacy of available land supply relative to projected demand. These techniques include: survey of landowner intentions, exclusion of development in process from the available land supply, ALSIS compatibility with the multiple listing service, classification of development potential by zoning type and subarea, identification of land availability by forecasted time of availability, tracking of sales prices over time, and increased accuracy of demand projections.

Governments must have good land supply estimates to relate to projected demand and to policy choices. Public and private sector perspectives on what constitutes "available" land supply often differ, and can lead to conflict over interpretations of ALSIS data. Governments usually view available land as vacant, physically unencumbered, serviced by infrastructure, and properly zoned. Private interests, on the other hand, would not view such land as "developable" if it was not available for purchase or development or if the land was not economically feasible to develop. In approximately one-third of the surveyed jurisdictions there was a conflict between the government's and private sector's definition of land supply available for residential development. Private sector criticism of monitoring systems argues that they overestimate the amount of land supply actually available to builders. In jurisdictions which actively manage growth through official policies, such overestimation can lead to the overconstraining of developable land supply and to land and housing cost inflation.

The goal of a monitoring government should be to arrive at a definition of available land supply agreed on by both private interests and the government. The following seven methods and techniques can help in this task by: 1) the refinement of the usual public sector definition of available land supply so that a "truer" estimate of land supply is possible, and 2) the measurement of the adequacy of available land supply relative to projected demand.

1. The monitoring jurisdiction should conduct an annual survey of

landowners of vacant, residentially-zoned land to determine their intentions regarding selling or developing. Governments often assume that all vacant, physically unencumbered, residentially-zoned land serviced by infrastructure is a commodity available for development or sale to would-be developers. This assumption does not apply to the real world of landowners, developers, and housing contractors. Not all landowners are willing to sell or develop their lands at "the right price"; some have reasons for wishing to retain their lands in their present uses rather than making their property available as a commodity.

In order to achieve an estimate of the amount of available land supply, the jurisdiction could hire a private consulting firm or a university-based research center to annually survey a stratified random sample of vacant land owners to determine their intentions. The results of a well-designed sample survey could be formulated into a factor that could be applied to total vacant land supply to estimate the "available" supply at that time. This technique will decrease the tendency of the government to overestimate the amount of land supply actually available for residential development. Figure 5 shows an illustrative format for summarizing data on available land supply.

Gruen Gruen & Associates, in their 1982 study of residential development in Stockton, California, conducted a survey of landowner intentions which can act as a model for governments interested in such surveys. Questions were asked of landowners to determine whether vacant land was available for development, and included the following:

- What are your major reasons or motives for holding the land?
- Is real estate your primary business?
- Have any previous proposals for development of this site fallen through?
- At present, can this property be considered available for development?
- If it is not available now, are you willing to seriously consider a sale or lease within five years?
- Why do you think the property is not likely to be put on the market or developed in the near future?
- Would any of the following effect your decision to develop or your development timetable? (options include change in market conditions, change in planning or zoning policies, and improved financing climate)
- What would you or have you been willing to sell or lease the property for?

	High Demand Areas	*Low Demand Areas*	*Total*
Holding capacity of land on which additional units could be built: 1980-90 (assumes all vacant land is available)	12,130	16,310	28,440
Percent of land likely to be available* for residential development	76.65%	27.64%	48.59%
Units potentially buildable on available land, 1980-90	9,300	4,510	13,810

Reasons given by landowners for not being willing to sell or develop their lands for any price included:

- desire to maintain active farms

- desire for privacy obtained by keeping large lots for personal residential use rather than subdividing whenever possible

- personal use of land for animals

- institutional use with desire to retain potential for institutional expansion

*Based on a survey of a randomly selected stratified sample of owners of land that is designated as residential in the General Plan.

Figure 5. *"Availability" of vacant land: A comparison of holding capacity approach with the survey-derived estimate of Stockton's in-fill potential: 1980-1990. (From Gruen, Gruen & Associates, "The Need for Housing and Additional Land for Residential Development in Stockton," January 1982.)*

- Referring to the current zoning of the subject property, how would you rate the market for this site?
- Over the next five years, do you believe the market for this property will improve, stay the same, or weaken? (Gruen Gruen & Associates, 1982)

2. ALSIS should track current ("pipeline") development and subtract acreage where there is development in process from the available land supply. If current development in progress and future permitted development are not subtracted from land supply estimates, ALSIS

will over-estimate the amount of land actually available to builders. Such "pipeline" acreage is not available to area developers and should not be included in estimates of available land supply.

3. Compatibility of ALSIS with computerized Multiple Listing Service (MLS) files should be encouraged. This will increase the relevance of system information to private sector users. Linking of ALSIS and MLS will provide private sector users of ALSIS with an indication of the percentage of vacant land supply which is actually "on the market" at a given time. Supply of available land, when viewed relative to demand, would increasingly be perceived by government as a dynamic, economic process, rather than as a static, spatial concept.

4. Development potential of vacant land supply should be broken down by zoning type in each subarea, and compared to demand projections by housing type in that subarea. The absolute supply of vacant land in a subarea is not necessarily a measure used by area developers in determining the suitability for development. Each subarea should contain enough developable land parcels to accommodate the projected demand for each type of housing. An example of this technique of estimating land supply by potential housing type is the Montgomery County (MD) Land Data bank System (see Figure 6). Dwelling unit potential for each policy area is broken down by zoning and potential structure type, and further classified by sewer service availability. These dwelling unit potential figures are then compared to demand projections to determine for each subarea whether enough vacant land supply exists in each of the zoning categories to meet projected demand. This technique provides a good measure of the adequacy of vacant land supply by examining the supply-demand relationship by zoning type.

5. The monitoring jurisdiction should attempt to identify land availability in terms of when it might be developed based upon present and future public and private actions. The estimation of local land supply in a given time period should be based on the understanding that the degree to which a given parcel of land possesses certain vital characteristics will determine how close that parcel is to being available for building. Such characteristics include zoning, infrastructure (planned, existing), physical hazards (absent, present), intention of landowner to sell or develop, and public actions on the parcel (proposed and approved rezoning, subdivision, special permits, and building permits). By examining the characteristics of a parcel, it would be possible to estimate the time period in which the parcel will become available for building. By adding the areas of parcels of land displaying combinations of characteristics associated with a particular

Zoning by Structure Type	Categories 1-3		Categories 4 & 5		Total	
	Units	Acres	Units	Acres	Units	Acres
Large Lot	10	15	20	60	30	75
RE-2	–	–	20	60	20	60
RE-1	10	15	–	–	10	15
Medium Lot	1,120	630	200	130	1,320	760
R-200	850	517	200	130	1,050	647
R-150	270	113	–	–	270	113
Small Lot	3,200	851	1,030	50	4,230	901
R-90	1,140	397	–	–	1,140	397
R-60	1,670	416	–	–	1,670	416
RT	390	38	–	–	390	38
PRC	–	–	1,030	50	1,030	50
Garden	2,910	161	1,030	301	3,940	462
R-30	130	9	–	–	130	9
R-20	1,140	63	–	–	1,140	63
PRC	1,640	89	1,030	301	2,670	390
High Rise	1,550	42	–	–	1,550	42
RH	1,550	42	–	–	1,550	42
Totals	8,790	1,699	2,280	541	11,070	2,240

"Structure Type" refers to large lot, medium lot, garden, etc. "Zoning type" refers to RE-2, RE-1, R-200, R-150, etc. "Categories" refer to sewerage service availability. Owners of land in categories 1-3 may apply for a sewer service authorization. Land in categories 4 and 5 is programmed for sewerage service in the future.

Figure 6. *Dwelling unit potential on vacant land by sewerage service category and type of housing—Kensington Policy Area, Montgomery County. (Source: Montgomery County Planning Board, "Land Supply and Demand—Sixth Growth Policy report," November 1980.)*

time period, it would be possible to estimate the total amount of land likely to be available in that time period. The projections of the temporal demand for land (based on demographic and economic analyses) would then be compared to the estimation of supply in matched time periods. This technique emphasizes the time-dependent quality of the supply/demand relationship and provides for a dynamic analysis of supply relative to demand.

6. ALSIS should include data on recent sales dates and prices. Such data should be routinely entered by the assessor's department. Land price monitoring is essential because the analysis of price over time is one of the few analytical means of determining whether a given land supply is adequate relative to demand. Scientifically sound methodologies for measuring annual changes in land and housing

prices should be developed. Land price indices should focus over time on standardized parcel characteristics so as to control for the effects of location, size, infrastructure, and neighborhood externalities. Housing price indices, in addition, should control for housing type and characteristics. The land and housing price indices should meet these additional criteria:

- Provide data in sufficient detail to be usable by public and private decision makers. Price information should be disaggregated by factors of: time, submarkets, and land use and intensity.
- Be sound methodologically so that decision makers and private interests can have reasonable confidence in the indices and their utility.
- Be economical to construct and maintain over time (Goldberg, 1980).

The price indices can be developed either from the sales data component of ALSIS or by periodically surveying real estate experts in the area. The advantage of using ALSIS sales and assessment data is that it can be used to construct jurisdiction-wide land and housing value maps which would pinpoint those subareas undergoing high price inflation. An example of the survey technique is the Urban Land Institute's "Residential Land Price Inflation Survey" of local appraisers, assessors, builders, and developers (see Figure 7). The monitoring government could hire a private consulting firm or a university-based research center to do such a survey.

7. The monitoring jurisdiction should be cognizant of the problems inherent in housing demand forecasting, and should work to improve the accuracy of these projections. Population projections, based on economic forecasts, often involve a range of uncertainty. The forecaster should acknowledge this uncertainty by providing different growth scenarios based on the adjustment of key variables. The art of scenario building should be viewed as the quantification of attitudes and social trends, not as a science. Key forecast variables subject to fluctuations over time include:

- Construction amount, type, and density
- Household size of in-migrating households
- Housing turnover rate
- Birth rates

The government should critically evaluate any tendency to extrapolate from the past the rates of these variables. These variables are affected by economic conditions, tastes, and social trends. The

I SMSA

II RESPONDENT'S INFORMATION (optional)
A. Name
B. Firm
C. Address
D. Telephone number
E. Check this box if you would like to receive a copy of the results of this survey. ☐

III RESPONDENT'S PROFESSION
_____ Assessor   _____ Appraiser   _____ Builder

_____ Developer   Other

IV SINGLE FAMILY RESIDENTIAL LAND PRICE ESTIMATES
Please provide estimated prices for each of the two types of standardized property described on the preceeding page. Be sure to read the parcel characteristics carefully before filling out the form. It is very important that your estimates are for residential land which closely meets the stated criteria. Only this will allow comparison of residential land costs between metropolitan areas. We would also like to know what is the typical size of a single-family detached home lot if it is not 10,000 square feet. Please enter this information on the separate entry line provided. Do not feel obligated to provide estimates if you do not feel qualified to do so.
A. Standardized Improved Single-Family Residential Lot (10,000 square feet)

   1985 Estimate $_____/lot
B. Standardized Unimproved Acreage Suitable for Single-Family Residential Use

   1985 Estimate $_____/acre
C. Typical Single-Family Detached Residential Lot (if 10,000 square feet is not typical of your area)

   Size_____square feet   1985 Estimate $_____
D. Check if not qualified. ☐

V SINGLE-FAMILY RESIDENTIAL LAND SUPPLIES
The following questions are designed to obtain a preliminary understanding for your region of public policies and actions that affect the supply of land for single-family detached housing. Information on demand factors will be obtained from other data sources. All of the supply questions are of a judgmental nature. We want your impressions. After a question you will find a bar line with subtitles that allow for a range of responses. Please clearly mark a space on the line that corresponds to your opinion. Circle no opinion only if you can not make a judgement.

A. Approval Times
   Has the time it takes to obtain a routine single-family project approval (zoning and subdivision) changed during the period from 1980 to 1985?

shortened considerably	shortened some	no change	increased some	increased considerably	no opinion

   How long does it take for a routine project approval in 1985?

under 3 months	6 months	9 months	12 months	over 15 months	no opinion

B. Zoning
   How would you judge the current adequacy of the quantity of land zoned for single-family lots in the range of 7,500 to 12,500 square feet?

excessive amount	more than needed	sufficient	shortage	major shortage	no opinion

   Has the adequacy of land zoned for residential lots from 7,500 to 12,500 square feet changed during the period from 1980 to 1985?

improved significantly	improved modestly	about the same	worsened somewhat	worsened substantially	no opinion

Figure 7. *Urban Land Institute's Residential Land Price Survey, 1985.*

PROPERTY TYPE ONE:
Improved Single Family Residential Lot

Characteristics

Size: approximately 10,000 square feet
(± 1000)

Zoning: single family detached

Location: —suburban fringe
—within 15-20 minutes driving
time of a major employment
center (not necessarily the
central business district)
—within 2 miles of an existing
grade school or bus zone

Development Rights: No restrictions other
than zoning and
building requirements

Utilities to Lot: sewer, water, electricity,
telephone

Neighborhood:
—not a high prestige area (home
prices in middle-range of new
home prices for area)
—area at least 50% developed
—no unusual conditions which
might impact the land price
such as:
 • significant pollution (air,
 water, noise)
 • environmental hazards
 (floods, etc.)
 • close proximity to amenities
 such as major parks or
 shopping/neighborhood
 services

Financing: The price should
reflect normal
financing terms for
your area

PROPERTY TYPE TWO:
Unimproved Acreage Suitable for
Single Family Residential Use

Characteristics

Size: 20-100 acres

Zoning: Residential, suitable for single family
detached development

Location: —developing fringe area
—within 15-20 minutes of a major
employment center (not
necessarily the central business
district)

Development Rights: No restrictions other
than zoning
subdivision and
building requirements

Utilities to Property: Connections to network
available at negligible
cost

Other Characteristics:
—not a prestige area (home prices in
middle range of new home prices for
area)
—no unusual physical attributes such as
slope or soil conditions which would
increase the cost of development
—no unusual environmental conditions,
e.g. significant pollution or hazards
—no unusual amenities such as
extremely close location to a major
shopping or recreational area

Financing: The price should reflect normal
financing terms for your area.

Figure 7 *(cont.)*

household size factor, in particular, has shown its tendency to vary in size in the past. Careful examination of these factors is crucial for good demand forecasting.

It is also useful to forecast housing demand by subarea and housing type. Such demand figures can be compared to supply calculations by potential housing type and subarea to determine the adequacy of land supply in each subarea. It is essential that common subareas be used for both supply and demand calculations. King County (WA.) uses a two-step method of subarea demand forecasting. After an economic base model generates totals of expected future population, households, and employment for the region, an activity allocation model (AAM) distributes the aggregate regional forecasts to smaller subareas in the region (King County, 1979). A second example of forecasting disaggregated by subarea is the City of San Diego's urban development modeling (Bamberger, 1980). There are three major components: the regional growth model, the spatial allocation model, and the microallocation model. The regional growth model links six economic and demographic factors by combining econometric equations with a demographic submodel. The spatial allocation model then distributes growth throughout the region according to specified growth assumptions, development constraints, and transportation. The aggregate regional forecast is allocated to 130 zones in the region. Finally, the forecasts for the zones are further allocated to 17,000 92-acre grids. Although the accuracy of the forecasts diminishes as the relevant geographical areas are reduced in size, the grid data are useful for aggregating to such larger geographical areas as cities, special districts, and community planning areas (supply data in San Diego is maintained at this level).

Both the King County and San Diego forecasting models are computerized, facilitating the entering of revised assumptions or updated historical data. The computer programs used by San Diego are in the public domain and could be installed on any large computer facility. Although the forecasting model is transferable, it does require extensive data requirements and the model components must be calibrated for each region. This requires a technical staff knowledgeable about economics, statistics, demographics, and geography, as well as computer applications.

For those evaluating the need to implement computerized forecasting models, a major question to ask concerns the worth of the system. Urban models are expensive and require a substantial amount of time to develop and gain credibility. In addition, inherent in the model system is the potential for misuse (Bamberger, 1980). At times, planners have had a tendency to take the models too literally rather than view them as what they are—simplified views of the real world. On the other hand, the application of a computerized forecasting model can provide sound estimates of demand to compare to the amount of vacant and available land supply tracked by ALSIS. The positive effect of improved supply data will be lessened if demand projections are based on faulty assumptions or inadequate data.

G. Users and Uses of ALSIS

Through the vacant land inventory, the city has documented that the amount of available land is currently greater than what the city needs each year to maintain General Plan objectives.

Tom MacRostie
Principal Planner
San Jose Planning Department

One-third of the system's benefits will flow to the private sector.

Dennis Barry
Contra Costa County Planning
Department

Once the private sector becomes aware of the system, high use is expected. This will undoubtedly elevate the level of discussion between government and private interests.

Gerardo Canto
Director, Office of Housing and
Neighborhood Development
City of New Haven

The system is becoming recognized as an objective accountant of land use trends in San Diego.

Max Schetter
San Diego Chamber of Commerce

Formatting and summarizing of land supply data should be designed to meet the needs of ALSIS users- both public and private sector. Cross-classification of vacant land by subarea and zoning type will increase ALSIS usefulness as a long-range planning tool. Dwelling unit poten-

tial should be computed by zoning type and compared to demand projections broken down by type of housing. Private interests will benefit from the parcel file, which will facilitate searches for land, and from the permit file, which can indicate the degree of development saturation occurring in specific subareas. Realtors, developers, marketing analysts, appraisers, and planning consultants can benefit from ALSIS use. One of the most important potential benefits of ALSIS will be the elevation in the level of discussion between government and the development community.

Potential uses and users of ALSIS land supply and project data include both public and private sector applications. Computerization allows diversity in formatting and summarizing of land supply data. This section examines several of the numerous possible applications of ALSIS data, and shows illustrative formats for summarizing parcel and project file data to meet the needs of ALSIS users.

Public Sector Applications

Long-range planners can use ALSIS to document the amount of vacant land by subarea and zoning type in the jurisdiction. This will provide essential information during General Plan updating, and improves the chances that vacant land supply will be better matched with demand forecasts. Figure 8 shows a format which classifies vacant land acreage by subarea. For each subarea, net acres of vacant land, percentage of subarea that is vacant, and percentage of vacant land in the city within the subarea is documented. Figure 9 is an example of vacant land classification by zoning type.

Cross-classification of vacant land by subarea and zoning type will increase ALSIS usefulness as a long-range planning tool. Figure 10 shows vacant land acreage by planning subarea and zoning type. In addition to tracking raw acreage, it will often be useful for long-range planners attempting to provide adequate vacant land supply to track dwelling unit potential by subarea and zoning type. Dwelling unit potential is based on existing zoning. Figure 11 shows dwelling unit potential on vacant land by zoning type for a specific planning subarea. Dwelling unit potential for the subarea can be compared to demand forecasts in the subarea for each type of housing to analyze the adequacy of the capacity of existing zoning to meet projected demand. Figure 12 shows a pie chart disaggregating a planning subarea by dwelling unit potential and zoning type.

ALSIS project data on pipeline, ongoing development can be an important source of land use trends for current planners, and can be used

SUBAREA	Total Jurisdiction		Vacant Land			For Each Land Use Category		
	Total Gross Area	% of Jurisdiction	Net Acres	% of Subarea	% of Vacant Land	Net Acres	% of Subarea	% of Land Use
WESTERN								
Area 1								
Area 2								
Area 3								
Area 4								
.....								
EASTERN								
Area 5								
Area 6								
Area 7								
.....								
NORTHERN								
Area 8								
Area 9								
.....								
SOUTHERN								
Area 10								
Area 11								
.....								
TOTAL JURISDICTION								

Figure 8. Land supply: vacant land and land use by subarea. (Adapted from San Diego Population and Land Use Bulletin, April 1984.)

ZONING CLASSIFICATION	Total Jurisdiction		Vacant Land			For Each Land Use Category		
	Total Gross Area	% of Jurisdiction	Net Acres	% of Zone	% of Vacant Land	Net Acres	% of Zone	% of Land Use
RESIDENTIAL								
Single-family								
Zone A								
Zone B								
Zone C								
Zone D								
. . . . .								
Multi-family								
Zone E								
Zone F								
Zone G								
. . . . . .								
COMMERCIAL								
Zone H								
Zone I								
. . . . .								
INDUSTRIAL								
Zone J								
Zone K								
. . . . .								
AGRICULTURAL								
MISCELLANEOUS/OTHER								
TOTAL JURISDICTION								

Figure 9. Land supply: vacant land and land use by zoning classification. (Adapted from San Diego Population and Land Use Bulletin, April 1984.)

Planning Subarea

ZONING CLASSIFICATION	Area 1	Area 2	Area 3	Area 4	Area 5	Area 6	Area 7
RESIDENTIAL							
Single-family							
Zone A							
Zone B							
Zone C							
Zone D							
. . . . .							
Multi-family							
Zone E							
Zone F							
Zone G							
. . . . .							
COMMERCIAL							
Zone H							
Zone I							
. . . . .							
INDUSTRIAL							
Zone J							
Zone K							
. . . . .							
AGRICULTURAL							
MISCELLANEOUS/OTHER							
TOTAL JURISDICTION							

Figure 10. *Land supply: vacant land acreage by zoning classification and subarea. (Adapted from Fairfax County, VA, Urban Development Information System.)*

For Planning Subarea 6 – Vacant Land

RESIDENTIAL ZONING CLASSIFICATION	Total		Infrastructure Committed or Existing		Infrastructure Proposed		Infrastructure Not Committed or Proposed	
	Units	Acres	Units	Acres	Units	Acres	Units	Acres
SINGLE-FAMILY								
Zone A								
Zone B								
Zone C								
Zone D								
Zone E								
. . . . .								
MULTI-FAMILY								
Zone F								
Zone G								
Zone H								
Zone I								
. . . . .								

Figure 11. Land supply: dwelling unit potential by residential zoning classification and infrastructure availability. (Adapted from the Sixth Growth Policy Report, Montgomery County Planning Board, 1980, and the 1976 Local Policy Survey, Association of Bay Area Governments.)

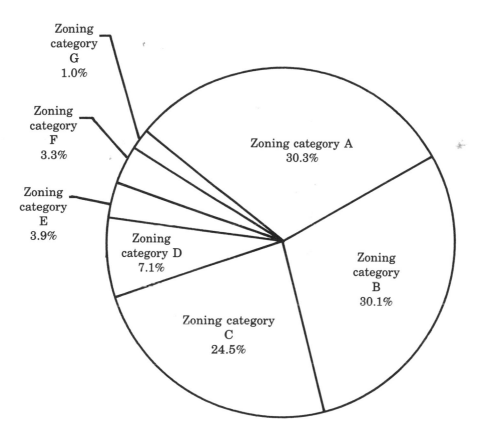

Figure 12. *Dwelling unit potential on vacant land for planning subarea 1. (Adapted from the Sixth Growth Policy Report, Montgomery County Planning Board, November 1980.)*

Number of Residential Units if Fully Developed
According to General Plan = 1,650

	Number of Residential Units	*% of Buildout*	*Accumulative Number of Residential Units*
EXISTING CONDITIONS			
Single-family			
Multiple-family			
Total			
UNDER CONSTRUCTION			
(Impact = Present-1 Year in Future)			
Single-family			
Multiple-family			
Total			
FINAL MAPS–APPROVED (Impact = 1-3 Years)			
. . . . .			
FINAL MAPS–CONSIDERED			
. . . . .			
TENTATIVE MAPS–APPROVED (Impact = 1-5 Years)			
. . . . .			

TENTATIVE MAPS–CONSIDERED

. . . . .

REZONINGS–APPROVED

. . . . . .

REZONINGS–CONSIDERED

. . . . .

SPECIAL PERMITS–APPROVED

. . . . .

SPECIAL PERMITS–CONSIDERED

. . . . . .

TOTAL IMPACT FROM PRESENT THROUGH
5 YEARS IN FUTURE
Single-family
Multiple-family
Total

Figure 13. *Impact analysis of pipeline development for Planning Subarea 17. (Adapted from Community Planning Areas Impact Report–San Diego Urban Information System, March 1984.)*

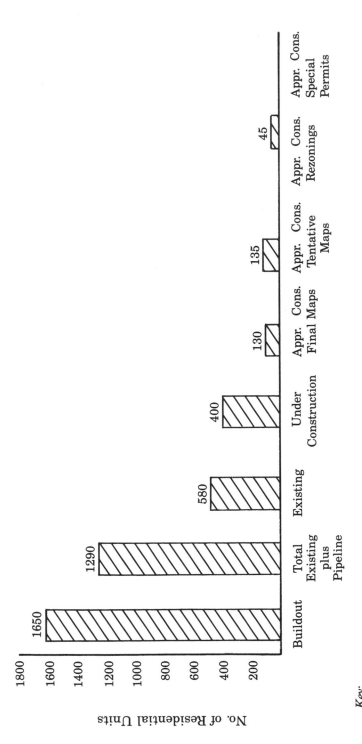

Key:
Buildout: Number of residential units if fully developed according to current zoning.
Pipeline: Under construction (+) final subdivision maps (+) tentative subdivision maps (+) rezonings (+) special permits.
Appr.: Approved.
Cons.: Considered.

Figure 14. *Impact report summary bar chart for Planning Subarea 17. (Adapted from Community Planning Areas Impact Report—San Diego Urban Information System, March 1984.)*

to compare existing and planned development to buildout potential in each subarea. This will provide planners with documentation regarding the adequacy of existing zoning in a subarea to meet demand, and will alert planners to upcoming deficiencies in land supply in specific subareas. Figure 13 shows the forecasted effect of current development and public actions on the number of residential units in a specific subarea. For each type of project or public action, residential units are estimated and compared to full buildout potential of the subarea. Time horizons are also used to forecast the year that the project or public action will affect the subarea. For instance, the effect of residential units under construction is forecasted to be from the current date to 1 year in the future, final subdivision maps are forecasted to affect the subarea between 1 and 3 years in the future, and the effects of tentative subdivision maps and rezonings are forecasted for between 1 and 5 years in the future. Figure 14 shows a summary bar chart of pipeline development impact, relating the number of residential units forecasted from existing and pipeline development to the total number of residential units if the subarea was fully developed according to current zoning.

As discussed in the previous section, ALSIS parcel sales data can be used to analyze land and housing prices over time by subareas. Such an examination is one of the few analytical means (although indirect) of determining whether a given land supply is adequate relative to projected demand.

In areas which have been largely built-up, such as New Haven, parcel data by subarea can be used to analyze housing and neighborhood activity. Comprehensive data on neighborhood change (especially ownership patterns) can be combined with data on economic activity to demonstrate to lenders the positive change in an area which warrants greater lending.

Private Sector Applications

The users and uses of ALSIS parcel and permit file data should not be limited to the public sector. Government should be advised on the kinds and formatting of data that the private sector needs during discussions with the leaders of private organizations (such as the Homebuilders' Association, Realtors' Association, or Chamber of Commerce) in the design phase of ALSIS. Potential uses of land supply data by the private sector are many and varied. ALSIS can perform a major role in helping private interests obtain more accurate and comprehensive information on vacant land supply and current development trends. As Figure 15 shows, many of the types of information commonly included in market studies would be found in ALSIS. The system would be an important source of information for analyzing supply, demand, site, and area characteristics. Private interests would be able to locate needed data in one automated system, rather than retrieve it through the many diverse sources traditionally used.

Private sector benefits from ALSIS include, but are not limited to, the following examples. The parcel file of vacant land parcels can be used as an exploration tool by developers and builders to find out how many vacant parcels with certain desired characteristics are located within a specific subarea. Case study interviews with private interests show that parcel file information is often used as a "lead-finder," as a good starting point in the search for land fitting the needs of the firm. Inclusion of assessor's data such as age of structure, construction type, and number of bathrooms would facilitate housing market analysis, and increase the use of the system by appraisers needing comparable properties for analysis. Parcel file information on landowner name and mailing address will facilitate contact by realtors and developers interested in purchasing the property. Developers wishing to build on a specific parcel can find out more easily with ALSIS which special districts serve the parcel. In California and other western states, user fees vary widely between special districts and this can have an effect on whether a project will be built or not.

The private sector will also benefit from the ALSIS permit file. The permit file's tracking of pipeline development by subarea provides realtors, marketing analysts, and developers the ability to document the market potential in a given area for a proposed development. As Figure 16 shows, permit file information could be used as an "inventory barometer" by private interests. Development firms searching for good locations to build will be assisted by ALSIS tracking of current development and public actions. By examining current and pipeline development, a private sector analyst can get an idea of whether a specific subarea is becoming oversaturated with the specific building type offered by the development firm. In addition, development firms can use ALSIS permit tracking ability to keep track of competitor firm activity in specific subareas. A computerized permit file will also likely increase efficiency and speed up the development review process, in addition to enabling faster government response time to private sector inquiries concerning project status.

Data on current rezonings and subdivisions provide developers and realtors important information regarding parcels which might be attractive to purchase. For example, a development firm specializing in multi-family development projects can keep track of recent rezonings

Information Needs	Traditional Data Sources	Included In ALSIS
Regional Urban Analysis		
Regional economic activity	Federal Reserve district banks	NO
Economic base analysis	Major financial institutions	NO
Population analysis	State economic agencies	YES
Income analysis	Census Bureau	NO
Growth and development patterns	Chamber of Commerce, University research centers, state real estate research centers, city planning depts., state and local depts. of highways	YES
Site Analysis		
Zoning/building codes	Local planning depts. and commissions	YES
Utility	Local utility companies	YES
Access	Local highway dept.	YES
Size and shape	Plat records	YES
Topography	Survey, soil samples	YES
Demand Analysis		
Competition	Survey, market knowledge	YES
Demographic	Census Bureau	YES
Trend Analysis	Building permits, starts, zoning change requests	YES
Supply Analysis		
Vacancy rates/rents	Survey, local appraisers	NO
Starts and bldg. permits	Building permits, starts, zoning change requests	YES
City services	Survey, planning dept.	YES
Community planning	Planning department	YES
Construction cost and financing	Local builder, financial institutions	NO

Figure 15. *Market study information found in ALSIS. (Adapted from Alvin L. Arnold, Charles H. Wurtzebach, and Mike E. Miles, Modern Real Estate, Boston: Warren, Gorham, and Lamont, 1980.)*

| | | | | | Status/Number of Units | | | | | |
Tract No.	Area/ Location	Developer/ Development	Acres	Density	Built	Under Const.	Final Map	Approved Map	Planning Stage	Notes*
PLANNING SUBAREA 5										
Single-family Large Lot										
....	400 S. Hale	R & H Builders	14.9	15.2				226		
....	1600 La Honda	Leary-Schmidt	21.0	2.8			59			Recorded 2/9/85
Medium Lot										
....	151 Rincon	James A. West	3.2	14.7					47	Submitted 7/20/84
Small Lot										
....										
Garden										
....										
High-Rise										
....										

*Including such items as date of recording, whether property is for sale, or permit status and date action taken.

Figure 16. "Inventory barometer": subdivisions. (Adapted from MPSI Systems, Inc., MPSI Residential Housing Survey, March 1985.)

and subdivisions of parcels in specified areas. Those multi-family rezoned parcels or subdivided parcels which look attractive to the firm could then be pursued for possible purchase in the future. Large realty firms can examine parcels which have final or tentative subdivision maps looking for opportunities to buy those properties which fit the needs of the realtor's clients. Landowner name and mailing address are part of the permit file, thus facilitating contact by interested realtors and developers.

Probably the most important benefit of ALSIS to the development community will be the ability to independently use system information to document the amount of vacant and available land supply in the total jurisdiction or a subarea of the jurisdiction. Such an analysis could be done by the Chamber of Commerce, Homebuilders' Association, Realtors' Association, or independent consulting firm. Private sector-derived supply estimates could then be compared to projected demand to determine the adequacy of the present land supply. A monitoring system which includes a definition of available land supply agreed on by both private interests and the monitoring government will be recognized as an objective and practical accountant of land supply. ALSIS would then be an important tool in bringing together public and private interests in the analysis of the adequacy of existing available land supply. Indeed, one of the most important potential benefits of ALSIS is the elevation in the level of discussion between government and the development community.

IV

Implementing an Automated Land Supply Information System

Four factors that can assure the successful implementation and operation of an ALSIS are discussed in this chapter. They are: gaining and maintaining political support for system development, using a steering committee to bring together data users and providers, evaluating work flow and assessing needs, and the modular staging of the implementation process. The following recommendations regarding the implementation of an ALSIS are derived mainly from discussions with personnel in the six case study jurisdictions.

A. Political Support

Political support for the system developed in the early 1970's due to our need to forecast future land use and land supply.

> Bob Davis
> Program Manager—Metro Council
> St. Paul, Minnesota

In order to get approval for the system in the first place, management had to understand its benefits. Once management understood, they liked the idea, and agreed to its development.

> Gary Ziegenfuss
> City Planning Department
> Sacramento, California

The education of management and the Board of Supervisors as to the uses of the land information system will be important in the future.

> Philip Batchelor
> County Administrator
> Contra Costa County

Agencies which incorporate innovations into day-to-day operations do so as much, or more, because innovations serve political rationality as technical rationality.

> Kenneth Kraemer
> "The Politics of Model Implemen-
> tation," in *Systems, Objectives,
> Solutions* 1 (1981), page 174.

Political support is vital to any serious ALSIS effort. It must be shown that ALSIS will be an important factor in public and private sector decision making.

Increasing Political Acceptability for ALSIS Development

Designers of an ALSIS must be aware of means by which an ALSIS development proposal can gain in political acceptability. Two aspects, in particular, should be emphasized: the system as a decision-support tool and as a benefit to the private sector.

Building political support for the ALSIS will not only generate resources to start up the system, but also will lessen the chances of funding cut-backs in the future. Political support is vital to having the power and resources needed for setup and operation. The importance of achieving and maintaining political support for the system cannot be over-emphasized.

It will probably increase the political acceptability of system development if a modular approach to development is taken. Periodic expansions and modifications to the system can be scheduled in the future, thus spreading out the overall cost of the system. Presenting the system as one package, rather than as a series of modular enhancements over time, would dissuade many decision makers because of cost considerations. Since the cost of all of the desired specifications in the full package may seem prohibitively high, it will often be best to prioritize the specifications and implement the system in a modular fashion, based on an assessment of relative costs and benefits for each of the modules.

It may also make the ALSIS more politically acceptable to fund only the development of the monitoring system through the General Fund, and have individual user departments responsible for funding operating costs through their budgets. This will make policy makers feel less burdened by the system's overall cost.

It will be important in the design stage to stress to decision makers those aspects of the ALSIS which will be potentially beneficial to them. For instance, it would be a good idea to stress to policy makers that the proposed monitoring system is not simply an operational or informational tool, but will also be a *decision-support* system assisting in the making and revision of policies.

In addition to the government benefits that can be derived from the ALSIS, policy makers should be made aware of the potential private sector benefits from the system. Such benefits include increased access to government information, and a more efficient development permit review process due to the permit tracking module. These possible private sector benefits from the monitoring system would provide the decision maker with a strong rationale for accepting the system proposal. Private sector involvement during the initial stages of ALSIS planning and development will increase political support for the system concept. A public/private consortium during the planning stage would consolidate support for ALSIS. Private sector representatives should at least include leaders from the Homebuilders' Association, Realtors' Association, and Chamber of Commerce. Private sector contributions for development of the system would increase the chances of ALSIS design approval by concretely showing private sector support for the system.

Designers of ALSIS should stress to public decision makers the biggest cost savings of ALSIS. Land and housing cost inflation due to over-constraining of land supply will tend to be avoided due to better tracking of land supply. In addition, better monitoring of existing and planned development will help avoid the excess public expenditures of unneeded or inefficient capital investment.

Benefits of an ALSIS

With the manual system, current planners would spend about two hours every morning answering public inquiries about particular projects or public actions from the day before. The computerized information system has cut this out almost completely and requests are now handled immediately over the phone.

Dennis Barry
Contra Costa County Planning
Department

The system more than paid for itself in its first program application.

> Gerardo Canto
> Director, Office of Housing and
>   Neighborhood Development
> City of New Haven

The King County (WA) computerized system demonstrates "how planning agencies hit by hard times can become indispensable by producing accessible data that can be easily updated."

> American Planning Association
> Award for outstanding planning
>   project, 1985
> (honorable mention)

We are selling the computerization idea by stressing the advantages——time savings, better updating, and personnel savings.

> Bob Johnson
> Research Section, Planning
>   Department
> City of Phoenix

Benefits of an automated system should be clearly detailed and broken down by user department. Types of benefits derived from an automated system include: cost savings, cost displacement, cost avoidance, and value added. Benefits will evolve over time, as opportunities evolve and expand with increased familiarity with the system and its capabilities.

The major benefit of an ALSIS is higher quality information for planning, policy formulation, and decision making. To facilitate implementation, it is necessary to show each user how this will benefit them specifically.

Policy makers will desire information on the benefits of developing and operating an ALSIS. Department heads will desire information on the benefits of operating and maintaining the system. Benefits of system development and operation (total, and broken down for each user department) should be clearly presented to policy makers as part of the proposal for system development. The feasibility report for the Contra Costa County system, for example, forecast first year cost savings in the planning department to occur in the following areas: updating of application status list ($7,852), front counter calls ($6,648), graphics updating of parcel pages ($6,512), and building permit processing ($5,318). By analyzing the cost effectiveness of the ALSIS, system applications in support of planning and policy analysis can be compared for relative value against the more common operational applications of automated systems, such as finance and accounting.

An aggressive effort should be made to quantify and justify both direct and indirect benefits of having a monitoring system. Positive effects of a monitoring system should be broken down into two categories: cost savings dollars and benefit dollars. Cost saving dollars are the cost difference to operate the proposed system rather than the present system over time. Benefit dollars typically fall into three categories:

- Cost displacement (reduction): an identifiable current expenditure, which will no longer represent a recurring expense because of the implementation of the proposed system.
- Cost avoidance: an identifiable planned or future expenditure which will not be made because of the increased productivity or efficiency resulting from the implementation of the proposed system.
- Value added: a dollar value placed on those less tangible gains normally illustrated through improvement in service delivered, planning and forecasting capabilities, or response to fluctuation in work volume, available because of the proposed system.

In estimating ALSIS costs to balance against benefits, several considerations should be kept in mind. First, most costs associated with the monitoring system will be continuing, not one time costs. On-going operational expenses, user training, and confidence building measures will probably be the largest cost item in the long term, so care must be taken not to underestimate these important long-term costs. Backup and restoration of the database are important items in systems which update daily, and hence require daily backups. These costs should be budgeted or the system will fail due to inability to meet unexpected operational problems (power failure, hardware and software problems, and telecommunications failures).

B. Steering Committee

Inter-departmental coordination can be a problem because data is often gathered for different purposes by different departments.

Jeff Bates
Office of Research and Statistics
Fairfax County, Virginia

An ALSIS steering committee should be formed prior to the design of the system. Such a committee would be composed of management-level representatives of proposed user departments in government and representatives of major private sector interest groups. The steering committee would be assisted on technical issues by task force groups composed of technical personnel from the proposed user departments. During implementation of the system, the steering committee should assure that all tasks being performed are in line with the conceptual design of the system.

An ALSIS steering committee should guide the design and development of the monitoring system rather than being formed after the design stage (See Figure 17). All proposed user departments and major private sector interest groups should be represented on the steering committee during the design phase.

Public sector representation on the steering committee should be management level personnel (such as departmental administrative assistants or assistant directors) because budgetary and personnel changes will be required by the introduction of an automated land records system. Without management level commitment during the design phase, important budgetary and inter-departmental questions will probably go unresolved, to the detriment of the system's operational stage later. Private sector representation should include leaders of the Homebuilders' Association, Realtors' Association, and Chamber of Commerce. For an effective public/private ALSIS, it is essential that localities be advised during the design stage on the kinds and formatting of data that the private sector needs.

Working with the management-level committee should be middle-level subcommittees (or task forces) composed of technical staff within the proposed user departments and groups. These subcommittees would work on the technical details of the system, such as land use coding, property identifiers, name standards, and cartographic information. Proposed day-to-day users of the system should be well represented on these subcommittees so they are involved in the design of the system's procedures.

Alongside the management-level committee and the technical subcommittees, there should be a single "system coordinator" or "system administrator" responsible for the system development and operation. This person would be the staff consultant to the steering committee during the design phase. The system coordinator and the data processing department representative should report to the steering committee to coordinate the varying needs of the committee members/depart-

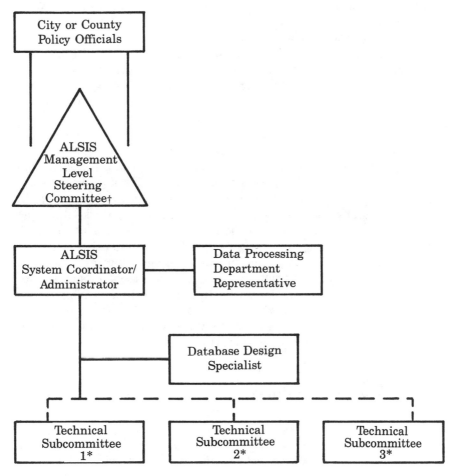

† *Steering Committee is composed of (1) government management level person-nel (dept. administrative assistants or assistant directors); (2) representatives from major private interest groups (homebuilders, realtors, chamber of commerce)*

* *Technical subcommittees work on a specific task (land use code standardiza-tion, property identifiers, name standards, etc.) and are formed as needed. Membership is made up of technical staff within proposed user departments, and proposed day-to-day users of the system.*

Figure 17. *Recommend organizational structure for ALSIS design and development.*

ments. The steering committee can better set priorities for development if they are made aware of the costs and benefits of particular features proposed for the system.

After the development of the system, the role of the steering committee should be one of assuring that all tasks are in line with the conceptual design of the system. The steering committee should be just as active in the implementation and operation phases of ALSIS as it is in the design and development stages.

Although the steering committee approach should be used whenever possible, there will be some situations where such an organizational structure may actually impede the establishment of an ALSIS. New Haven, for example, spent years trying to develop a mainframe system. Steering committees set up were found to be too unwieldy due to the presence of many competing priorities. What finally worked for New Haven was the assigning of prime responsibility to one department (The Office of Housing and Neighborhood Development) and the setting of a deadline for design and implementation. However, this example appears to be an exception. A steering committee approach worked successfully in Charlotte, Contra Costa County, and San Diego. Many interviewed jurisdictions which had not used a steering committee during the design stage stated that they wished they had done so to assure inter-departmental coordination.

C. Work Flow Evaluation

To have an efficient and effective computerized system, you just can't automate an existing manual system, but have to modify the manual system's content and procedures. If you don't do this, manual inefficiencies will become automated inefficiencies.

> Tim O'Connell
> System Coordinator–UIS
> San Diego Planning Department

An understanding of pre-existing operational activities in the proposed user departments should form the basis for establishing ALSIS functional requirements. The needs and requirements of user departments should be incorporated into the automated system design as much as possible. ALSIS automated procedures, however, should not necessarily be an exact clone of pre-existing procedures because manual inefficiencies may become automated inefficiencies.

One of the first tasks in implementing an information system should be an examination of existing work flows. At this step, extensive interviewing and data gathering from potential user departments and groups should seek to understand how the current operational activities (prior to the information system) are performed. These interviews with user departments should be aimed at acquiring the following information:

- *Organization and Responsibility*: the primary functions performed by each agency or unit.
- *Tasks and Systems*: the key tasks employing or developing land-related information and the manual and/or automated systems currently used in these tasks. The dependencies among tasks and systems, and the flow of data through those systems. Hardware and software currently employed for automated systems (if any) and the data associated with the tasks.
- *Data Sources Used and Generated*: land related data items developed and used by the organization, including existing formats, display media, extent of data coverage, size of files, frequency of use, data accuracy, as well as data management procedures and geocodes.
- *Observations*: general observations regarding the problems experienced with respect to accessing, using, and referencing land-related data.
- *Needs and Wants*: functions not now automated but desired to be automated, as well as other ways of improving the use of land-related information.
- *Information System Potential*: agency's assessment of potential utility of applying information system's automated procedures to the functions of the agency. Interviewer's assessment of potential utility.

This analysis of existing work flow and needs can be done either by an outside consulting firm or in-house by system analysts. Upon completion of the interviews, the analyst would then determine and define the automated system's functional requirements. These requirements would include data types, software, and hardware required to support the observed tasks and organizational interactions examined during the interviews.

Functional requirements of user departments should be incorporated into the design of the automated system as much as possible. Data entry tasks which are extraneous to a department's role or mission should not be assigned to that department because incomplete records will in all likelihood result.

It is important to realize that the ALSIS should not necessarily be a clone of the existing manual and/or automated procedures. Inefficiencies that existed in the manual system would tend to be copied into the automated system's procedures. A time management study of the inter-agency flow of work before automation would decrease the possibility that manual inefficiencies will be copied by the automated system. Such inefficiencies would be duplication of work effort across departments, or inefficient fragmentation of work tasks across or within departments.

An objective of the ALSIS should be replacement or modification of the existing manual procedures, not adding on to manual work another layer of data capture. The system should be designed so as to benefit the person with a file in his hand. If the system adds another layer of data capture on top of the existing manual process, assigned employees may be careless because the extra data won't be something they depend upon for their day-to-day work. In addition, the more ALSIS procedures become incorporated into day-to-day work, the more assurance that critical ALSIS data entry tasks will not be curtailed during periods of fiscal austerity.

D. Staging Implementation

A modular approach to implementation should be used because it will spread out front end costs (thus increasing political acceptability), add to system flexibility, and lead to concrete "success stories" in a brief time. An overall design should guide the acquisition of incremental enhancements so that consistency and compatibility are assured between the different system components. Implementation should proceed first within the government, dealing with problems of transition. Once organized, the ALSIS should consider means of improving private sector access to the data.

There are important benefits from using a modular (incremental enhancement) approach to ALSIS development. First, it spreads out the front end costs of the system and thus increases the chances of funding. Political acceptability is increased because the presentation of the system as one package, rather than as a series of modular enhancements over time, would tend to dissuade many decision makers because of cost considerations. Second, it increases the flexibility of the system and its ability to adapt to changing user needs and technology (hardware and software) in the future. Finally, modular implementation will tend to satisfy expectations of early payoffs, and will provide the implementing government with tangible and early evidence of system benefits.

In a well designed modular implementation strategy, each enhancement of the system is planned so that it will be easily linked with existing components of the system. In addition, initial components of the system (such as hardware and software) are acquired which will be compatible with future enhancements to the system. It is important when using a modular approach to have an overall design agreed on for the future. If there is no overall blueprint in the background guiding future expansions, the total system cost may actually increase over that which was forecasted as future adaptations may require costly restructuring of the database. The key here is to "design holistically, but implement modularly."

Once a recommended design solution has been agreed upon by the steering committee, there should be a refining of the concepts of database, hardware, software, and organizational/management structures to comprise the system. Along with a final design solution, there should also be a conceptual implementation strategy explaining the various implementation steps.

Initial commitment to the procedures outlined in the final design solution is an important first implementation step. From this point on, all data collection and information system development should be done in a manner consistent with the eventual ideal system, as decided by the steering committee. Standardization of addresses, land use codes, and other data field coding should be figured out before data collection and entry begins. Also at this stage, all parcel-level data should begin to be coded with both assessor's number (or other property tax identifier) and local address (if it exists). The system coordinator/administrator should be responsible for seeing that all developments are compatible with the eventual ideal system and that all programs developed are documented and publicized across departments. Where possible, it may be a good idea at this stage to commit to technology enhancement rather than increased staff.

With the initiation of an automated system there come possible feelings of intimidation and displacement on the part of staff members in the user departments. Steps should be planned ahead of time that will alleviate some of these adverse effects. All user departments should be allowed "free computer time", and "hands-on" computer work should be encouraged. Training sessions given by government employees who are computer literate should be set up to assist in the diffusion of computer know-how and to lessen possible feelings of intimidation concerning computerization.

Assuring the continued growth of the ALSIS database during the initial implementation stages should be on the mind of user department directors and assistants. Every "funded" land-related project should be seen as an opportunity to add data to the system. The use of the system to solve specific problems should be publicized across departments so that others will begin to see ways that the system might be helpful to them. If data gaps appear during the initial implementation stages, it may be necessary to make personnel or budgetary changes to close these gaps.

Once sufficient data have been automated, the implementing government may want to appoint an individual to be in charge of facilitating private sector usage of the system. Methods to improve or increase private sector use of the system should be considered. A private sector oriented system documentation manual could be produced and regularly updated. Initial private sector users could be invited to all public training programs dealing with the logistics of accessing the system, data sources, features and functions, and benefits. At first, private sector access to ALSIS information could be assisted by government employees at a public counter so that initial private sector experience with the monitoring system would not be frustrating. Eventually, however, government may want to move in the direction of private sector on-line access, with possible downloading of subsets of the total database. If private sector on-line access is desired, the government should initially advertise the availability and potential uses of the system to centralized private sector organizations (Boards of Realtors, Chambers of Commerce, Local Development Corporations, Homebuilders' Associations). This makes economic sense for private sector users, and will help "spread the word" about the potential benefits of the ALSIS to the private sector. As stated earlier, user charges for private sector on-line access should initially be based on marginal cost pricing should occur after substantial private sector acceptance of the ALSIS.

As the ALSIS database grows and routinization of automated procedures occur, it is recommended that a computer mapping system compatible with the existing information system be acquired (budget permitting). X-Y coordinates should then be added as the third identifier in the system (in addition to situs address and assessor's parcel number). Digitization can often be a time consuming job, so it is recommended that the government look into the possibility of contracting with a service bureau to do this work.

E. The Evolving Nature of an ALSIS

The system is 10 times more complex and useful than when the feasibility report was done.

Dennis Barry
Contra Costa County Planning
Department

The system has taken on a life of its own.

Gerardo Canto
Director, Office of Housing and
Neighborhood Development
City of New Haven

The creation of an ALSIS can be represented by four phases: planning, analysis and design, implementation, and operation. Different components of a system will each go through these four phases, but not necessarily at the same time. It is best to think of system design and operation as dynamic and subject to change, and to maintain flexibility in system plans.

So far, we have emphasized the design and implementation phases of an Automated Land Supply Information System. These two phases are probably the most crucial because management approval is essential to the system's survival during these two phases. However, one should view these phases as part of a larger "system life cycle" (Stern and Stern, 1985). This life cycle is represented by four stages:

1. *Planning:* development of a plan or course of action and establishment of project control guidelines; consideration of resource and time constraints.
2. *Analysis and design:* analysis of the existing work flow and user objectives and constraints; identification of data requirements and coordination of data-element definition and related requirements of the various users; design of the new system.
3. *Implementation:* establishment of a procedure for beginning, maintaining, and modifying the new system; assuring that there are no major transitional or conversion problems; user orientation is a major activity.
4. *Operation:* periodically review efficiency and effectiveness of the new design, making sure that the new system functions properly.

Even the "life cycle" above does not give a true picture of the system's evolution. These four phases do not occur neatly one after the other, but rather overlap as different components of the system are in different phases at the same time. For instance, the parcel file component may be in operation at the same time that the project file component is being designed or implemented. The key is to consider possible system components and anticipate future modifications during the initial analysis and design phase to the extent possible, so that compatibility is assured and system disruption is avoided in the future.

System design and operation are best viewed as dynamic and subject to change. Interviews with all six of the case study jurisdictions in this study brought out the evolutionary nature of their systems, and the often unexpected changes the systems have undergone. An ALSIS will probably need to be continually revised to better meet new and changing objectives. Modifications or "fine tuning" will be necessary from time to time to ensure that the system continues to function even if objectives and goals change. An ALSIS master plan should be flexible enough to allow for system modifications due to changing objectives, new user department requirements, or the introduction of new kinds of computer equipment on the market.

V

References

Bamberger, William J., "Urban Development Modeling: San Diego Case Study," in Kraemer, Kenneth L. and John L. King (eds.), *Computers in Local Government: Urban and Regional Planning*, Auerbach Publishers, 1980 (with supplements).

Barnard, Charles and Walter Butcher, "Landowner Characteristics as Determinants of Developer Locational Decisions," paper presented at AAEA meetings in Clemson, South Carolina, July 1981.

Black, Tom and Jim Hoben, "Land Price Inflation and Affordable Housing: Causes and Impacts," *Urban Geography*, 1985.

Bouchard, Robert F., and Justin D. Franklin (eds.), *Guidebook to the Freedom of Information and Privacy Acts*, Clark Boardman Company, 1980 (with 1982 supplement), Appendix C: State-by-State Freedom of Information Statutes.

Canada Mortgage and Housing Corporation, Land and Infrastructure Division, *The Land and Infrastructure Mapping Program*, January 1980.

Dowall, David E., "Reducing the Cost Effects of Local Land Use Controls," *APA Journal*, April 1981.

Dowall, David E., *The Suburban Squeeze: Land Conversion and Regulation in the San Francisco Bay Area*, University of California Press, Berkeley, 1984.

Dowall, David E. and Jesse Mingilton, *Effects of Environmental Regulations on Housing Costs*, Council of Planning Librarians, Bibliography #6, May 1979.

Dueker, Kenneth J., "An Approach to Integrated Information Systems for Planning," in Kraemer, Kenneth L. and John L. King (eds.), *Computers in Local Government: Urban and Regional Planning*, Auerbach Publishers, 1980 (with supplements).

Einsweiller, Robert, "Increasing the Supply of Land in the Fringe Area," in HUD, *Reducing the Development Costs of Housing: Actions for State and Local Governments, Proceedings of the HUD National Conference on Housing Costs*, 1979.

Epstein, Earl F. and William A. Chatterton, "Legal Issues in the Development of Land Information Systems," *Wisconsin Land Information Newsletter,* Vol. 2, No. 2, 1984.

Gleeson, Michael E., "The Effects of an Urban Growth Management System on Land Values", Hubert Humphrey Institute of Public Affairs, Research Applied to National Needs Program, National Science Foundation, 1978.

Goldberg, Michael A., "Developing an Urban Land Price Index Model: Models, Methods, and Misgivings," in Black, Thomas and James Hoben (eds.), *Urban Land Markets: Price Indices, Supply Measures, and Public Policy Effects,* ULI Research Report #30, 1980.

Graaskamp, James A., *A Guide to Feasibility Analysis,* Society of Real Estate Appraisers, 1970.

Graaskamp, James A., "Identification and Delineation of Real Estate Research," *Real Estate Issues,* Vol. 10, Number 1, Spring/Summer 1985.

Gruen, Gruen & Associates, "The Need for Housing and Additional Land for Residential Development in Stockton," January 1982.

Gruen, Gruen & Associates, "LandTrak: The Tri-Valley Land Use Database," unpublished, 1985.

Horwood, Edgar M., "Planning Information Systems: Functional Approaches, Evolution, and Pitfalls," in Kraemer, Kenneth L. and John L. King (eds.), *Computers in Local Government: Urban and Regional Planning,* Auerbach Publishers, 1980 (with supplements).

Huxhold, William E., "Automated Systems for Building Permits Processing and Housing Code Inspection Reporting," in Kraemer, Kenneth L. and John L. King (eds.), *Computers in Local Government: Urban and Regional Planning,* Auerbach Publishers, 1981 (supplement).

Hysom, John and Stephen Ruth, "A Nationwide Assessment of Local Government Planning Information Systems," Center for Real Estate and Land Use Analysis, School of Business Administration, George Mason University, Fairfax, Virginia, October 1983.

King County Department of Planning and Community Development, "King County Supply-Demand Study, Part I: Capacity of Existing Zoning," April 1979.

Kraemer, Kenneth L., "The Politics of Model Implementation," *Systems, Objectives, Solutions* 1, 1981.

Landis, John, "Land Regulation, Market Structure, and Housing Price Inflation: Lessons from Three California Housing Markets," *APA Journal,* forthcoming.

Metropolitan Council of the Twin Cities Area, *Development Framework Policy, Plan, Program,* 1975.

Montgomery County (Maryland) Planning Board, "Land Supply and Demand—Sixth Growth Policy Report," November 1980.

National Association of Realtors, Economic and Research Division, *Profile of Real Estate Firms,* 1984.

Nelson, Arthur, "Evaluation of Urban Containment Programs," PhD dissertation, published by the Center for Urban Studies, Portland State University, 1984.

New Haven Office of Housing and Neighborhood Development, "Pilot Neighborhood Analysis: Using SOLIR Software Package", November 1983.

New Haven Office of Housing and Neighborhood Development, "Managing Municipal Information Needs Using Micro-Computers: Conference Summary and Background Materials," October 4-5, 1984.

People for Open Space, "A Resource Manual On Assessing Residential Land Availability", Technical Memo #2, 1983 (512 Second St., San Francisco, CA 94107).

Portland Metropolitan Service District, "Urban Growth Boundary Findings," 1979.

Real Estate Research Corporation, *Infill Development Strategies*, published by APA Planners Press and Urban Land Institute, 1982.

San Diego, City of, "City Progress Guide and General Plan, Draft Housing Element Revision" (currently being considered), 1985.

Segal, David and Srinivasan, Philip, "The Impact of Suburban Growth Restrictions on U.S. Housing Price Inflation 1975-1978," unpublished, July 1980.

Seidel, Stephen R. *Housing Costs and Government Regulations: Confronting the Regulatory Maze*, The Center for Urban Policy Research, 1978.

Spurr, Peter, "The Canadian Land and Infrastructure Mapping Program," in Black, Thomas and James Hoben (eds.), *Urban Land Markets: Price Indices, Supply Measures, and Public Policy Effects*, ULI Research Report #30, 1980.

Stern, Robert A. and Nancy Stern, *Computers and Information Processing* (2nd ed.), Wiley and Sons, New York, 1985.

Urban Land Institute and Gruen, Gruen & Associates, "Effects of Regulation on Housing Costs: Two Case Studies," 1977.

Wurtzebach, Charles and Mike Miles, *Modern Real Estate* (2nd ed.), Wiley and Sons, New York, 1984.

Appendix A

Case Studies

Contra Costa County, California: Land Information System (LIS)

Background

Contra Costa County's Land Information System (LIS) went on-line in January of 1983. The first formulation of LIS needs occurred in 1979 due to difficulties with the assessor's batch system. These difficulties included: revenue not collected quickly enough, building permits not entered in a timely fashion, and adjacent owners not notified of public action fast enough. The county also wanted to increase efficiency between departments by providing a common database, and to provide better service in the development permit process.

Heights Information Technology Service, Inc. was hired by the County in 1980 to produce 2 feasibility reports for an automated land development information system. Based on recommendations of the consultant study, a steering committee was established and charged with development of LIS. The following departments were represented on the committee: Building Inspection, Planning, Public Works, Assessment, Data Processing, and County Administrator's Office. Committee members were largely management-level personnel (such as Administrative Assistants and Assistant Directors) because of the need to make policy and budgetary changes during the design stage. Smaller subcommittees were formed to work out technical aspects of the system. All government interviewees during the case study stressed the importance of having a steering committee during the design stage of the system, and all said that LIS was well designed to meet the needs of user departments because input from the departments was included in the design phase.

In FY 1981-1982, the County Board of Supervisors funded the development of LIS for $150,000. The LIS project has expended the following amounts for development of the system (these do not include operating costs):

1981-1982: $ 58,000
1982-1983: $295,000
1983-1984: $348,000
1984-1985: $795,000 (development of 2 major additions to LIS)

Sources of funding for the development of LIS include the General Fund, state funding of supplemental assessor's role development, and permit fee money.

The LIS database includes approximately 280,000 records of existing and retired parcels (all parcels in the unincorporated areas and some parcels in incorporated areas) and is on a IBM mainframe computer located in the Data Processing Department. The database is accessible to numerous government departments through the use of interactive mainframe software. Computer programs for the system were written in-house by Data Processing personnel. The database is maintained and updated by all four land development departments: Assessor's, Building Inspection, Planning, and Public Works. All of these departments, plus Data Processing and the Administrator's Office, were represented on the LIS steering committee and were part of the design phase.

Two LIS staff members, the Project Director and the DataBase Design Specialist, are responsible for answering questions from user departments and for doing preliminary analyses of modifications and enhancements of LIS. It is necessary for LIS staff to talk both the technical language of Data Processing and the practical language of the user departments. LIS staff is also the most involved with the assessor's department.

LIS is a relatively young system (3½ years old) and is thus still evolving. Two major additions/enhancements are scheduled for LIS in mid-1985. They are the Assessor On-Line subsystem and the Permit Management System (PMS).

System Elements

Hardware. The automated system combines features of a centralized and a distributed system. The entire database is on an IBM 4381 mainframe computer, and is accessible with interactive mainframe software. The LIS database is a subset of the assessor's records plus planning records which have been entered. ITT Courier terminals are used as access points to the centralized database. There are 42 Courier terminals in the Assessment Department, 19 in Building Inspection, 3 in Planning, and 6 in Public Works.

The distributive feature of LIS is the use of microcomputers in the Planning Department and the downloading of subsets of the full database onto the micro. Planning uses an IBM PC-XT with a 10 megabyte hard disk. Advantages that the Planning Department have found with the XT include the provision of customized data sets for individual users (subset of the full database, containing parcels having certain characteristics, for instance), speed of operation, less expensive computer runs, and increased editing capabilities. Examples of database subsets downloaded onto the XT include: list of land use permits that have expired, or are coming up for expiration, and a list of all Environmental Impact Reports up for review in the next month. Sorting of the full LIS database is too big an operation for the XT and interactive mainframe software is required. However, sorting of a subset of the full database can be done with the XT using vendor micro software. In addition to the Couriers, LIS staff also uses an IBM 3270 Personal Computer.

Software. Interactive accessing software for the mainframe database is structured so as to provide the user with menu driven commands. The database manager used on the mainframe is IDMS (manufactured by Cullinet). Multiple screens (see Parcel Information section below) are available to fit the needs of the various user departments. IBM Information Center software is used for report generation.

Software used by the Planning Department with the XT includes R-base 4000 and 5000, a database manager used for data manipulation and error checking. Planning has found R-base flexible and comprehensive, and can use R-base string commands to sort the database by at least 3 variables. R-base files are transportable to Lotus 1-2-3, and thus can act as a link between mainframe and micro applications. Lotus 1-2-3 is used for its spreadsheet capabilities in financial accounting and bond reporting, and for its report generation capabilities. Multiplan software package has also been used in the past.

The three XT's in Planning are used for 1) multi-purpose, 2) word processing, 3) financial accounting and bond reporting. The XT's are increasing the computer literacy of planners slowly. Of the 14 Planning staff members, it is estimated that 6 are 1-2-3 literate and 2 are R-base literate. Limited time on the job to learn micro software was cited as the reason for this.

Unit of Tabulation. The building block of LIS is the tax parcel, as defined by the Assessment Department. The basic units of aggregation are the Census Tract (for Planning), the tax rate area (for Assessment), and the supervisor's district (for Building Inspection).

Parcel Information. Information on all existing and retired parcels in the county includes:

Parcel number
Parcel history (public actions on that parcel)
To-From (showing 'parent' or 'child' parcel numbers)
Tax rate district (code designating each unique combination of taxing districts)
Primary and secondary owners
Land and improvement values

Situs description
Situs address
Notification address
Taxability code
Reason for latest valuation change
Census Tract
Supervisorial district
Seismic zone
Flood hazard zone
Land use code
Acreage
Drainage fee

Data elements available for all unincorporated areas of the county include the following. Member cities have the option to enter their own data in these elements.

Zoning
General Plan area and designation
Building inspection notice to comply
Permits for building inspection, planning applications, and public works permits (for further information on the Permit Management System, see Pipeline Tracking section)

The database can be accessed through any of 15 different screens (inquiries), each tailored to fit the needs of particular users. They include the following inquiries: assessor, planning, public works, building inspection, situs or owner, miscellaneous (permits by application type or census tract), professional, permit call-in, and zoning (detailing allowances under a particular zoning type, with notes/remarks for more detail).

A parcel can be accessed by situs address, parcel number, owner's name, permit number, and census tract.

Vacant Land Definition. There are three classifications of vacant land: unbuildable, 1 site, 2 or more sites (subdivided). The "unbuildable" classification is based on the particular land use policies of the relevant jurisdiction. "Unbuildable" can be due to slope, terrain, lack of sewer, flood zone, view, or noise (depending on a jurisdiction's policies). The land use code is entered by the Assessment Department.

Updates. All departments except Assessment update the LIS database on a daily basis. The parcel file currently is updated by Assessment on a monthly basis. This will change in July, 1985 when the Assessor On-line subsystem becomes active. At that point, information on new and retired parcels will be up to date. The Permit Management System (PMS), when active, will provide current information on the development review process for all projects. Data entry in the Planning Department is the responsibility of one staff member. Updating is done both in batch and on-line mode.

System Use

Outputs. Currently, there are no periodic summary reports produced from LIS by the Planning Department. The Building Inspection Department does produce a monthly summary of all Building Inspection, Planning, and Public Works permits, summarized by numerous geographic aggregation levels. Also, there are monthly summaries of inspection by type and inspection by geographic area. These monthly reports are done with IBM Information Center software and are remote batch processed.

Data Sources. Sources for data elements include: assessor's parcel file, zoning maps and ordinances, General Plan designation, Planning Department environmental maps, building inspection data, contractors information on file in Building Inspection, and public works data. Individual agencies enter the various data elements to create a common database which all agencies can then use. Data elements are tied together by parcel number, address, and owner's name.

Users and Uses. The County Administrators Office describes LIS as "more of an informational working tool for departments instead of a policy tool at this point". The main benefits of LIS so far have been increased efficiency and increased management capabilities. The main government users of LIS are (in order of use frequency): Assessment, Building Inspection, Planning, and Public Works.

Building Inspection uses LIS to track permits and inspections, to determine the amount of required developer fees based on the tax rate area code, and as a work load management tool. LIS has cut the department's manual work, and has been a valuable management and production tool.

Planning's use of LIS so far has been predominantly for current planning applications, not advanced planning. LIS has cut down on time in the initial phases of the development review process. Public requests concerning a parcel or project can now be handled immediately over the phone, rather than the next morning. At this point, Planning is not using LIS as an analytic tool, although this kind of use is scheduled to increase in the future. A hard copy of the LIS land use inventory is currently being used as the basis for manually producing updated county base maps. These maps will be used for the General Plan review process slated for the near future. It is estimated that the LIS-generated inventory probably saved 2-3 person years of work as compared to the previous base map project which relied heavily on field checks.

Future possible uses of LIS by Planning include statistical analyses looking for opportunities for low-income housing and other types of development. This could be carried out through sorting by area, land cost, ability to subdivide, and by figuring out "developability" criteria. Build-out potential for the county is not now being emphasized as a product of LIS. In the future, the system could be used for additional advanced planning applications, such as looking at carrying capacity limits and potential for build-out based on jurisdictions

involved and capital facilities. With the current General Plan being reviewed in the next two years, it seems inevitable that LIS will be increasingly used
to answer questions concerning the county's long-term growth potential. LIS
is a young, evolving system which will encounter more and more applications
as the years pass.

In addition to county government users, there are also six member cities
which have on-line access to LIS information on a user charge basis. Two examples of city use include:

San Pablo: computerized telephone hook-up with 3 access points (one each
in Building Inspection, Planning, and Police Departments). Building Inspection has benefited because they now are capable of more direct and up-to-date
retrieval of assessor's data.

Danville: Planning Department has used LIS to inquire about parcel history,
owner's name, and the permit process. Danville is currently entering their own
information, such as rezonings, development plans, variances, use permits, and
the political history of parcels (including violations). The provision of a
database already created by the county has benefited this young city which
has a small planning staff constantly occupied by current planning questions.

The county has set a user charge schedule for member cities which want
online access to LIS. User charge is $350/month for the first terminal and
$275/month for each additional terminal, plus a one-time setup charge of
$2000 (includes user training and technical assistance).

Private sector use of LIS has been growing over the years. It is estimated by
the Chief of Data Services in the Planning Department that "1/3 of the
system's benefits flow to the private sector". Comments from private sector interviewees include:

- LIS would best be used as an exploration tool, and as a source of
  background information.
- Board of Realtors is interested in the possibility of linking their com-
  puterized Multiple Listing Service with LIS.
- Commercial use of LIS evident, especially with larger brokerage houses.
- Centralized access points for the private sector (at Board of Realtors,
  Homebuilders Association, Chamber of Commerce, Local Development
  Association) would be most economical approach for individual developers
  and realtors.
- LIS information was useful for a development firm which did a market
  study for a commercial site, using LIS building permit counts to forecast
  future market potential in the area.

Budget. The Board of Supervisors funded the development of LIS through the
General Fund. Each user department funds operating costs through their own
budget. This method of funding increased the political acceptability of LIS

because the user departments would bear the responsibility for funding the system's operating costs.

The cost/benefit analysis done by Heights Information Technology Service, Inc. in October of 1980 estimated total annual operating costs to be $368,600 the first year of operation and $448,036 the fifth year of operation.

Access/Security. There is on-line access to the LIS database, with responses to queries shown on the terminal screen. Most computer programs are menu-driven, allowing the user to choose between different components of the system.

Access to on-line cities is by modem or hardwiring (dedicated lines), depending on distance.

Security is considered a strong part of the system. Three types of security are used. Terminal identification security will allow only certain terminals to retrieve LIS information (this is used predominantly to secure confidential information). Password security allows only certain users to access and/or update LIS information. Update security identifies which data elements can be updated or modified by whom (updater identified by terminal and password). Online cities are limited in their updating and modifying to certain parcel number ranges contained within their jurisdictions.

Pipeline Tracking. The Permit Management System (PMS) is scheduled for start-up in July 1985. Each stage of the planning application and building permitting/inspections process will be entered into the system as the action occurs. Two major objectives of PMS are

a. to provide Planning and Building Inspections Department with timely and accurate information for the purpose of processing and tracking planning applications and building permits.
b. to increase the efficiency with which permits and applications are issued and processed.

PMS will store data on a single mutually accessible database, will eliminate the duplicate entry of the same data, and will improve the accuracy of data used between departments. In addition, PMS aims at a more effective integration of the Planning and Building Inspection application and permit processing functions.

A permit in PMS will go through a stepped process of inputting. First, Planning Application Tracking will schedule and track the planning application. Next, the Planning Department will enter building inspections data pertinent to property characteristics. Next, Building Inspection will enter information concerning owner and contractor. Finally, Building Inspection will enter project characteristics such as square footage, usage, and fees (which are automatically computed based on tax rate area code). For each step, type of permit, action to be taken, date scheduled, date action taken, action taken (status) is tracked. When each step is complete, inputter "initials" screen, signifying the completion of the step. The final permit is not processed until all screens are "initialled" by appropriate personnel.

PMS will track applications and public actions such as rezonings, subdivision, special permits, and building permits. Features unique to PMS include the recorded history of the planning application process and the automatic generation of future review dates (based on California law, in many cases, having to do with maximum allowed public review times). Within the planning application tracking subsystem, a plan check log has also been designed for use on complex projects which have many steps and types of review.

Comments/remarks from public agencies can also be entered into PMS. A comment can be stored on a warning level, such that the comment will come onto the screen automatically when parcel or project number is called. A comment on "weak hold" can be overridden by a simple password, while a "strong hold" will require a stronger override. Comments section would be most beneficial in recording physical limitations or other factors which should preclude development on that parcel in the future. If special districts are on-line, they could enter their remarks about the property directly into PMS.

PMS is expected to speed up the permit issuance process, and increase applications management. This would be in conformance with state statute AB 884, which sets development process time guidelines and limits.

Private Sector Information System Relationship. County government plans to encourage private sector on-line access to LIS in the future. Real estate, title companies, development firms, and other businesses would be able to subscribe to the system on a user fee basis. Access would be through modem or dedicated lines (hardwiring), depending on distance. User charges have already been set by the county for private sector on-line access. User charge is $850 for the first terminal and $550 for each additional terminal, plus a $2000 one-time setup charge (which includes operator training and technical assistance).

Benefits to the private sector also will become apparent once PMS is on-line. Benefits will be largely in the form of a faster permit review and issuance process.

System Problems

Link to mapping is needed so that presentation of raw data will be facilitated. Tying parcel identification to invariant geographic identifiers (such as polygon) would increase ability to analyze the history of a parcel or area.

Documentation of interactive mainframe software is usually lacking or incomplete. This is especially important for on-line users of LIS outside county government. In-house computer programs are usually written in the face of a time deadline, and there is often not enough time for documentation.

LIS system is currently synchronized with the updated batch assessor's information on a monthly basis. This time delay in receiving new assessor's information (such as ownership changes or new parcel numbers) will be done away with when the Assessor On-line subsystem becomes functional.

Lack of a standardized procedure for entering situs addresses has led to varying ways of inputting the same street name (for instance, 123 Olympic W., 123 W. Olympic, 123 Olympic). This can lead to incomplete responses when doing sorts or searches. In May 1985, the Assessor established standardized entering procedures for addresses, so this problem should be minimized in the future.

Backup and restoration of LIS database has been expensive. When system is undergoing daily updates, it is necessary to back-up database daily, thus increasing costs. As of latest plans, PMS is not slated to be backed up due to cost considerations. This will lead to increased vulnerability of the PMS database.

"System is ten times more complex and useful than when feasibility report was done," according to the Chief of Data Services and Evaluation in the Planning Department.

There is potential congestion in Planning Department in the future, with regard to microcomputer use. Conflicts in scheduling the use of the three micros is possible, especially when word processing is one of the competing tasks. "Personal" has been taken out of Personal Computer because staff members do not have freedom of use and access to a PC on desktop. Due to budget constraints, Planning has only one multi-purpose PC.

There are potential capacity problems downloading subsets of the full database to microcomputer. Successful downloading will depend on the size of the subset, how many data elements make up a parcel record, how records are set up (do blank fields take up memory, for instance), and the amount of resident software on the hard disk.

Currently, the user charge for private sector on-line access ($850 for the first terminal) is such as to dissuade hook-ups by single firms. Centralized access points for the private sector (in Board of Realtors, Homebuilders' Association, etc.) may provide the answer to this problem.

There is relatively low computer literacy rate in the Planning Department. Staff should be trained to use the PC peripherals (such as R-base 5000 and Lotus 1-2-3) so that capabilities of system will be put to full use.

System Improvements

The Permit Management System will automate the tracking of permit processing (see Pipeline Tracking section).

Assessor On-line will provide an on-line facility for updating and maintaining three roll years worth of assessor's information throughout the fiscal year. The present scope of the new Assessor's On-line subsystem includes design and implementation of dynamic update function of all Assessor related information on the database, maintenance of a history of changes, and production of hard copy reports. With this new module, current types of updates (ownership changes, new parcels, etc.) will occur immediately and outputs relative to these updates may be produced immediately. Updated information can be accessed through different on-line inquiry screens which will greatly facilitate obtaining accurate, current information for the public and government users.

LIS staff may request for next fiscal year that a feasibility study be funded which would look at the possibility of a computer mapping module for LIS. Pacific Gas and Electric currently is beginning work on such a mapping system. Contra Costa County (and the hired consultant) would be able to learn from PG and E's current experience.

Faster mainframe computer will possibly be necessary in the future. The current 4381 is slower and older than the 3000 series.

Further Information

Publications. Heights Information Technology Service, Inc. "Automated Land Development Information System for Contra Costa County", October 30, 1980.

–"Functional System Requirements"
–"Feasibility Report"

Contact
Bob Nash
LIS Project Director
651 Pine St., 8th Floor
Martinez, CA. 94553
Telephone: (415) 372-2386

Dennis Barry
Chief- Data Services and Evaluation
County Planning Department
651 Pine St.
Martinez, CA. 94553
Telephone: (415) 372-2035

Fairfax County, Virginia:
Urban Development Information System
(UDIS)

Background

The Fairfax County Urban Development Information System (UDIS) is a mainframe computer information system that was developed to provide a consistent database for County planning and decision making. It records land information at the individual parcel level, combines it with Census and other data, and reports this information for geographic subareas within the County. UDIS information is available to the public primarily in published annual reports.

UDIS was begun in 1970 with a design and pilot test project that was funded by a $125,000 HUD grant and an in-kind contribution of $140,000 from the County. After a successful pilot test, additional federal funding of $226,000 and County funding of $244,000 was used to extend the system to the entire County. In 1973, UDIS became operational as a part of the new Office of Research and Statistics, where it provides a running inventory of land in the County.

The UDIS logic is based on a three phase process:

1. the system monitors growth and makes short term forecasts of housing and population by small areas.
2. the annual forecasts are translated into demand for public facilities.
3. demand forecasts are analyzed to project timing and location needs for new facilities.

One of the earliest land monitoring systems in the country, UDIS is now being considered for updating and redesign. In addition, it is now supplemented by several other County computerized information systems which focus on projects rather than on parcels and subareas:

1. the Rezoning Application System (RAPS) operated by the Office of Comprehensive Planning,
2. the Plan and Agreement Monitoring System (PAMS) operated by the Department of Environmental Management,
3. the Inspection Services Information System (ISIS) operated by the Department of Environmental Management.

Together, these make up a related set of land information systems.

Fairfax County Land Information Systems

System	No. Records	Transactions/Year
UDIS	250,000	25,000-30,000
RAPS	1,000	4,000-5,000
PAMS	250,000-300,000	850,000
ISIS	250,000-300,000	1 million

Besides the land project management-oriented information systems, UDIS also interfaces with the County's Real Estate Assessment and Billing System (REABS), Police Management Information System (PMIS), Public Works Sewer Application Tracking System (PUBSAT), and Water Authority Combined Billing System.

System Elements

Hardware and Software. UDIS operates on an IBM 3081 mainframe computer with 32 MEG of core memory. Its software includes SAS and EASYTRIEVE programs. It has limited small area mapping capability with SAS GRAPH, but does not have parcel mapping capability. The County is adding an automated mapping system, however.

Unit of Tabulation. The basic UDIS unit of tabulation is the parcel. Parcel data can be aggregated by several subareas: Supervisor District, Planning District, Sewershed, SubCensus Tract, and Subdivision.

Parcel Information. Besides the subarea identifier, parcel information provided includes:

Map reference number
Street address
Dwelling unit count
Land area
Existing land use
Zoning
Assessment
Building permit
Planned land use
Underutilized and vacant acreage
Stage of development
Site plan or subdivision plan
Rezoning
Gross floor area
Sewer identification

Updates. UDIS information from the tax assessor is updated annually, as of January 1 each year. Updates are started in March, using the assessor's tape, and completed and published in the annual reports sometime during the summer or fall. The assessor's tape is updated continuously throughout the year and then frozen at year end, when it is picked up by UDIS. Other information, such as permits, inspections, and occupancy, is updated at more frequent intervals, including daily for some files.

System Use

Outputs. UDIS was designed under a concept of central data processing and annual report issuance. More recent, separately developed, County land information systems tend to be oriented toward management of individual agency responsibilities, such as permit issuance or project review. For ongoing management purposes, these decentralized systems require updating and reporting on a current basis, rather than annually.

The primary UDIS output is a published volume titled the Standard Reports, which presents detailed data by subarea on the County's housing inventory, population, residential and nonresidential construction activity, nonresidential structures, planned and existing land uses, and household income. About 900 copies of the Standard Report are published each year.

A second published report is the annual Fairfax County Profile. The Profile reports on economic and demographic characteristics, such as income, age, race, employment, and housing. About 1500 copies are published annually.

UDIS also is used to produce annual reports on housing, commercial, and industrial development activity, as well as special reports on request, primarily for County officials. It has been used to provide data for the Annual Comprehensive Plan Review, and for studies of fiscal planning, water quality, sewer service, housing forecasts, highway corridor development, and land use litigation. Because Fairfax County's Comprehensive Plan uses a growth management approach to coordinate land use regulation, public facilities provision, and sensitive environmental area protection, UDIS information is important to planners and decision makers.

Vacant Land Definition. UDIS produces a report on Vacant or Underutilized Parcels as of January each year. Vacant parcels are those with no improvements or those containing dilapidated structures. Underutilized parcels are those whose current density is lower than their density planned under the Comprehensive Plan. This information is compiled on a parcel basis (on a printout) and on a small area basis (in the Standard Reports). Examples of these reports are shown on the following pages.

To illustrate the use of this information, assume that a developer is seeking the locations of vacant or underutilized parcels planned for high density use, over 20 dwelling units per acre, in a particular area of the County. He could look at the Standard Reports table above and see which planning districts contain such land and the overall total acres. He could then review the parcel listing to identify each individual vacant or underutilized parcel planned for a density of over 20 dwelling units per acre and locate these on a tax map.

Besides vacant and underutilized land, Fairfax County annually calculates the overall amount of developable land, excluding land that is in roads and water, planned for residential use within the County. It also provides small area estimates of "buildout", the number of dwelling units that could be built if the Comprehensive Plan were fully implemented. Buildout is calculated by

ACRES OF VACANT AND UNDERUTILIZED LAND
BY PLANNED LAND USE

SUPERVISOR DISTRICT

PLANNED LAND USE	CENTRE VILLE[1]	DRANES VILLE[2]	ANNAN- DALE	LEE	MASON	MOUNT VERNON	PROVI- DENCE	SPRING FIELD[3]	TOWN CLIFTN	TOWN HERNDON	TOWN VIENNA	TOTAL ACRES
RESIDENTIAL												
.1-2 DU/AC	100	1,876				225	27	722				2,950
.2 DU/AC		270				74		20,143				20,487
.2-5 DU/AC	950	4,920	23			2,714	175	2,268				11,027
.5-1 DU/AC	2,696	1,494			36	257	312	683	97			5,598
1-2 DU/AC	985	2,088	195	249	267	669	304	2,797		17		7,571
2-3 DU/AC	2,344	891	480	1,041	350	991	777	3,007		98	58	10,037
3-4 DU/AC	521	57	52	1,867	55	144	734	884		473	21	4,808
4-5 DU/AC	51	62	8	194	75	235	95	362		55		1,137
5-8 DU/AC	544	28	71	359	35	193	439	1,086		23	4	2,782
8-12 DU/AC	2	15	46	79	24	107	177	252		31	3	736
12-16 DU/AC	13	6		5	5	1	58	136				224
16-20 DU/AC	8		2	57	17	46	109	60		64	1	364
20+ DU/AC	50		7		10	5	46	143				261
MOBILE HOME				1								1
SUB TOTAL	8,264	11,444	1,147	3,852	874	5,661	3,253	32,543	97	761	87	67,933
COMMERCIAL/INDUSTRIAL												
COMM-OFFICE	38	29	14	388	66	70	573	632		7		1,817
COMM-RETAIL	98	155	19	95	42	114	101	150		61	3	838
INDUSTRIAL	3,113	276	36	828	2	661	130	2,289		188	24	7,547
SUB TOTAL	3,249	460	69	1,311	110	845	804	3,071		256	27	10,202
OTHER NONRESIDENTIAL												
PUBLIC PARK	742	1,126	136	254	63	1,852	191	2,476		47	20	6,907
PRIVATE REC	262	407	31	238	11	424	21	702		10	4	2,110
FLOODPLAIN	125	185	29	206	14	220	82	435			3	1,299
PUBLIC	243	103	66	221	50	91	68	145		2	2	991
> 2 USES	892	157		154	2	86	177	116				1,584
SUB TOTAL	2,264	1,978	262	1,073	140	2,673	539	3,874		59	29	12,891
TOTAL	13,777	13,882	1,478	6,236	1,124	9,179	4,596	39,488	97	1,076	143	91,076

Source: Fairfax County Office of Research and Statistics, *1984 Standard Reports.*

County of Fairfax: Vacant or Underutilized Parcels as of January 1984

Map Reference Number	Total Acres	Developed Acres	Vacant Acres	Under Utilized Acres	Primary Planned Use	Secondary Planned Use	Primary % of Total	Land Use	Zoning
0271 11 0002C	7.4297	.0000	7.4297	.0000	20+ DU/AC	–	100	Vacant	R-30
0544 01 0084	1.4090	1.0000	.0000	.4090	16-20 DU/AC	–	100	SF Detached	R-1
1044 01 0011	16.0450	.0000	.0000	16.0450	16-20 DU/AC	Floodplain	80	SF Detached	R-8
. . . .									
0262 01 0073A	2.3584	.0000	2.3584	.0000	20+ DU/AC	–	100	Vacant	R-30
. . . .									
0774 01 0032	13.6450	1.0000	.0000	12.6450	16-20 DU/AC	–	100	2 SF/lot	R-1

Source: UDIS Printout, January 1984.

adding the number of units that could be built on vacant or underutilized land to the existing residential units.

Data Sources. Data sources include construction records, building permits, rezoning cases, geographic identifiers from maps, water and sewer billing file, assessors file, and sanitary sewer network records. Within UDIS this data is maintained in six primary data files: 1. the parcel file, 2. the sanitary sewer network file, 3. the rezoning case file, 4. the building permit file, 5. the residential development process file, and 6. the non-residential development process file.

Users and Uses. The Office of Comprehensive Planning has used UDIS extensively in the preparation and annual review of the Comprehensive Plan. During Plan reviews, UDIS information allows elected officials to see the effects of the previous year's Plan revision decisions upon the development capacity of each part of the County, including their Supervisor District. Planners draw upon UDIS for historical trends and current status of land development and for base information for special studies. For example, the Office of Comprehensive Planning is conducting an Infrastructure Availability Study in cooperation with the Public Works Department, in which the adequacy of existing public facilities is being analyzed to see whether planned growth can be accommodated. It also is analyzing the availability of apartment sites for affordable housing in response to developer requests.

Many other County offices use UDIS data. It has been used for a political reapportionment study, for a school capacity analysis, for a legal defense of land use regulations, and for a water quality study. The Fairfax County Economic Development Authority uses the economic and demographic data from the Standard Reports to answer business client requests for information. County Supervisors' offices have terminals, but their use of UDIS for analysis has not been extensive.

Private developers tend to use UDIS for background information, and to rely on other County project information systems, such as RAPS, PAMS, or ISIS, to track projects through the government review and approval process. They also tend to subscribe to private information services which offer information not available from UDIS. The Sager Documaster system provides a computer-oriented microfiche service with a monthly update of site plan reviews as well as compilations of ownership and tax map information, mortgage data, master plan land use, and overlay restrictions. The Fairfax Newsletter provides a weekly report on building permits, rezoning requests and approvals, site plan and subdivision plat submittals and approvals. Both these private services pull their information from County sources.

Budget. The annual UDIS budget is not calculated separately from that of the Office of Research and Statistics. It consists of portions of various staff members' time and about $13,000 of computer time. A 1984 estimate of the annual cost of providing the population estimates (a part of UDIS) for the

County and its sub-areas totaled $37,800 (including $25,000 for demographic staff, $6,500 for household survey, $1,700 for programming, and $4,600 for computer charges).

Access. Access to UDIS for County government agencies is through written requests to the County Executive for data other than published reports. The availability of on-line terminal access would be useful to agencies such as the Office of Comprehensive Planning and the Economic Development Authority.

Private information services have arranged to acquire County computer tapes and updates. Most private users rely upon the annual published reports.

Development Process Tracking. UDIS does not track projects in the development process, other than through registering changes on an annual basis. More frequent tracking is done by other public and private information services.

System Problems

Most often mentioned problems reported with UDIS stem from its design as a batch processed, mainframe system which is limited to annual updates. These problems include lack of timely information and limited access to data. A second reported problem is the system's lack of integrated graphics and mapping capacity. A third problem named by some users is the system's tendency to focus on parcel and small area data, rather than on more analysis of larger trends; this is related to a perceived lack of effort to educate and inform potential users about the availability and interpretation of the system's information. (The Standard Reports do contain summary and time series data.) Finally, a number of smaller concerns include inability to enter by street address, lack of capacity to enter all land use data when there are multiple overlay districts, lack of information on allowable zoning (vs plan) density, lack of ownership information (which is available in the Real Estate File, though not in UDIS), and some failures to code land use accurately.

Both public and private UDIS users regret the time lag built into the development data in annual reports, which is some nine months old by the time it is published. They believe that making more current information widely available could help to reduce problems such as overbuilding of particular types of development. Private users also regret the stated County policy not to support requests from outside businesses or organizations that require County personnel to generate or reformat computerized data, except by special exception. They believe that the inflexibility of this policy reduces the usefulness of the data.

UDIS reports lack both graphic analysis and display in the form of charts and tables, and computer maps of land characteristics and trends. Users feel that the UDIS numbers need to be "translated", graphically and spatially as well as numerically, to illustrate their effects.

An interesting comment about UDIS is that it was designed during the period when Fairfax County was developing as a bedroom community for Washington employees, and that now that Fairfax County is becoming a major office and commercial employment center the lack of non-residential data in UDIS limits its usefulness for both public policy and market decisions.

Another observation about the limits of UDIS is its lack of integration with the capital budgeting process. Separating the Capital Improvement Program from the land information system prevents presentation of a clear picture of the effect of infrastructure on future growth.

There was general agreement that UDIS gives priority to County government needs. The system is not oriented toward the needs of developers and private users, except through the annual reports, and there is not sufficient staff to work with such users.

Given the size and complexity of Fairfax County government, which has some 6000-8000 employees not counting the school system, and the County growth rate of some 10,000 parcels per year, internal coordination is a major task. Different departments gather data for different purposes and using different definitions, not all of which have been coordinated under an overall database management concept. Constant care is required to avoid double counting.

System Improvements

The major planned improvement is the addition of a computer mapping system within the County's Division of Communications. This will provide the capacity to digitize base maps.

A comprehensive evaluation of UDIS has pointed out the need for updating. Expected changes include modernization of the system design to make it more efficient, to automate linkages with other systems, to enhance the database (with further information about land characteristics and public facilities), and to improve the reports within an overall database environment.

Further Information

Publications

John L. Hysom, Jr. et al. (1974) A Handbook for Creating an Urban Development Information System: A Foundation for Planning and Managing Growth. Office of Research and Statistics, Fairfax County, Virginia.

John L. Hysom, Jr. and Stephen Ruth. (1983) "A Nationwide Assessment of Local Government Planning Information Systems." Center for Real Estate and Land Use Analysis, School of Business Administration, George Mason University, Fairfax, VA.

Office of Research and Statistics. (1984) Computer System Abstract. No. 203. Fairfax County, Virginia.

Contacts
George Kohut, Branch Chief
Assessment and Land Use Branch
Office of Research and Statistics
4100 Chain Bridge Road
Fairfax, VA 22030
Telephone: (703) 691-2355

John Yeatman, Technical Supervisor
Office of Assessments
4100 Chain Bridge Road
Fairfax, VA 22030
Telephone: (703) 691-2379

Sidney Steele, Director
Office of Comprehensive Planning
4100 Chain Bridge Road
Fairfax, VA 22030
Telephone: (703) 691-3011

Lane County, Oregon:
Regional Information System (RIS)

Background

Since the Regional Information System (RIS) in Lane County has as its primary component one of the oldest and most fully developed geographic information systems in the country, more supporting documentation is included with this case study. Moreover, portions of several non-technical publications describing the area's economic condition are included because the current system's utilization can be fully understood only in the context of changing economic conditions. Finally, the evolution of the system was closely related to the extensive state level land use planning effort in Oregon and this fact must be considered when drawing generalizable conclusions from Lane County's experience.

RIS's geographic history is easily decomposed into two parts. The description of the period from inception in 1971 to the crest of the economic boom in the late 1970's is quoted from "Plotting Land Use in Oregon" by Mahan, Spivac and Swank in *Datamation*, November, 1978.

Early System Development

Lane County, a 4,610 sq. mi. area in the middle of the state, takes in the cities of Eugene and Springfield that sit on each side of the winding Willamette River. Almost half of its population of 252,500 lives in Eugene, which has grown over 30% over the last ten years to 104,000. In an area with such growth, information was needed to resolve issues such as:

- Where are sites with adequate land, water and transportation for future residential, commercial or industrial development?
- Where can the sheriff allocate patrol resources to provide better crime prevention?
- What impact will the development of land, already zoned for development, have on current public services?

Ten years ago the development of land use information for the Eugene-Springfield metropolitan area's master development plan and for the master transportation plan was done manually. It involved a tremendous data collection task in which a set of 750 tax maps depicting every parcel of land had to be collected and then organized by area and planned routes that would allow the viewing of all parcels with as little backtracking as possible.

The manual method was time consuming, inflexible and inaccurate, because it took so long from initiation to completion that significant changes could occur while the study still was going on.

The Geographic Data System project was started in 1971 when a comprehensive land use plan was being developed for the Eugene-Springfield metropolitan area. Preparation of the plan required a tremendous amount of data collection. To facilitate monitoring of the plan, and to support other planning processes such as transportation planning, a decision was made to create a computerized land use file.

Participants in the cooperative development were the Lane County Dept. of Regional Information Systems, the City of Eugene, and the Lane Council of Governments along with federal, state, and local agencies and departments. (The Regional Information System (RIS) is an IBM 370/158 AP-based facility that provides hardware and system software to public agencies in the county. It is being converted to an MVS operating system. Each department and agency provides its own programming expertise, but the system software and hardware resources are centralized in the RIS.)

Access to the information is in either batch or interactive mode. Reports and large plots can be produced in batch while queries can be made through alphanumeric or graphic terminals. Continuing input to the system comes from the operational files of various local government agencies and is coordinated by the Lane Council of Governments, a central agency. This arrangement is formalized in a Cooperative Project Agreement. Renewed every year, it specifies the project budget and the contribution of each agency, as well as project objectives.

After the decision was made to create a computerized land use file, several alternative systems were investigated, including a grid system and a system from the Census Bureau called GBF/DIME. It was decided that parcel, or point level, data could best satisfy the anticipated uses. To ensure data consistency, a composite of maps from the Lane County Department of Assessment and Taxation was used to create a computerized file of all ownership and land use parcels. In two years, some 750 maps were digitized, edited, and compiled into a complete parcel file containing land use data for the Eugene-Springfield metropolitan area. Each parcel file now contains 120,000 records and each record has 100 to 300 bytes.

The data collection effort took five man-years of work and was supported by a $50,000 grant from HUD and $30,000 from the City of Eugene and the Lane Council of Governments. In addition to the data collection effort, a system of computer programs—called the Map Model Systems—was acquired to process the data.

But by 1974, when the complete metro area parcel file was available, the original land use data was more than two years out of date. To protect the investment in the parcel file and to provide the current information necessary for planning decisions, a method was developed to maintain the tax lot, land use, and address information in the parcel file.

Other planning tools grew out of the early experience with the parcel file. In 1975, a programming team developed an on-line address cross-reference system. Shortly thereafter, a standardized file of boundaries (e.g., census tracts, precincts) was established. In 1977, an on-line system for zoning records was created for the Eugene Planning Dept. Other applications, such as tax assessments and records, are loosely tied to the Geographic Data System.

In 1973, when interest began to be expressed for the use of interactive graphics to provide simpler and faster map drawing services, an interactive mapping system using a Tektronix 4014-1 graphics terminal was developed. Then, in the fall of 1985, a Tektronix 4081 intelligent graphics terminal was purchased to improve these capabilities. A powerful digitizing/editing system was written using this device, and the map drawing system was rewritten for the 4081.

The Geographic Data System has two chief components—data, and the hardware and software tools which manipulate and display that data. The data in the Geographic Data System is identified and interrelated chiefly by geographic coordinates that define the location related to the data according to the Oregon State Plane Coordinate System. For example, a tax lot (ownership parcel) can be identified by assessor's map and tax lot number and by state plane coordinates which define the parcel perimeter and centroid.

The foundation of the geographic data base is the *Parcel File*. It contains the digitized perimeters of all land ownership parcels together with "parcels" for streets, rivers, and other features needed to make up a complete map. Each parcel record contains, along with the coordinates, a sizable amount of alphanumeric data: land use, acreage, zoning, property value, and the like. It is collected from a variety of sources and combined by either geographic or alpha matching with the original digitized parcels. It is the source from which other special purpose files are created, and it is used for drawing maps on the plotter.

Keeping the Parcel File up to date is an extremely important function. To date, uses have been almost entirely in planning. For the majority of these applications, data a year or two old has been acceptable, although this is changing. Therefore, the file is on an annual cycle for updates. Building permits are the main source of information on changes in land use. The process is coordinated with the annual update of the real property assessments and the assessor's maps. Changes in these hand-drawn maps are digitized for entry into the Parcel File. This results in the Parcel File being at least one year out of date at the time it is released each year.

An interesting problem that arose in the initial definition of the Parcel File was the distinction between the ownership and use of the land. For example, it is generally necessary to know that a certain tax lot contains both a residence and a store. It also happens that a single use, like a large warehouse, will span several lots.

The solution is to have three types of records on the Parcel File: 1) tax lots, 2) land uses, and 3) (the majority) tax lots having a single land use. Types 1 and 2, together, are overlapping polygons. However, 1 and 3, or 2 and 3, together would both form complete maps. The user must decide whether his/her data is needed by land use or by tax lot. Some types of data are only available by tax lot (e.g., land value), while others are available only by land use (e.g., number of dwelling units). This causes occasional confusion, but it seems to be a fact of life and not an artifact of system design.

The *Address Library (ADLIB) File* is a particularly useful derivative of the Parcel File. The Address File provides a standardized set of site addresses in Lane County, containing one record for each address. These records are maintained in an address sorted order by city, street, type, direction, and house number. Each record also contains the Oregon State Plane Coordinate point of address, the tax lot number of the parcel with which the address is associated, the land use at the address, the number of units (for residential parcels), the census tract, and the date the record was created or updated. The same information that is used to update the Parcel File is used to keep the file current.

Primarily a reference file, it can be used interactively through a display terminal or it can be processed in a batch mode. A clerk can quickly validate an address or a planner can fix the tax lot or land use for a specific lot by interrogating the file from an on-line display terminal.

The development of the Address File was aided by a Lane County project to re-address rural parcels and implement a consistent addressing scheme throughout the county. The Rural Re-Addressing Project, completed in 1976, eliminated the old route and box address system, and assigned a new address based on the Oregon State Plane Coordinate System. The new addresses contain a five digit number corresponding to the east-west or north-south state plane coordinate of the access point to the building, and the road name.

In addition to providing standardized addresses throughout rural Lane County, the system has greatly improved the ability to locate rural residences and has proven to be of particular value to fire departments, law enforcement agencies and other emergency service agencies.

The *Zoning File* contains zoning class information for the Eugene-Springfield metropolitan area. Zoning has not yet been completed for the entire county. The file is similar in structure to the Parcel File. Each zoned area is stored as a record which contains the state plane coordinates of the zoned area perimeter and a code for the type of zoning. It can be overlayed with the Parcel File to produce land use by zoning cross tabulations. In making a decision on a zone change request, government officials find it useful to know the surrounding zoning and land uses. For example, if a developer argues that there is insufficient undeveloped residentially zoned land in a particular area, the Geographic Data System can compile the exact acreages and locations of undeveloped residentially zoned land to determine the validity of the argument. The Zoning File is also used to identify and monitor nonconforming land uses within zoning classifications.

Many other computerized files have been created, including boundary files, files for soil types in the metropolitan area, the metropolitan sewer file and the street files.

The Lane County Dept. of Assessment and Taxation stores information on all real property in the county in a computerized data base. Interrelation of this data with other geographic data can be through the tax-lot number or site address. Real property data can then be aggregated by any desired area of analysis, such as census tract, city limits, special taxation district, etc. The real property information then can be analyzed and compared with other information.

The assessment data offers a wealth of periodically updated information. In addition to its value for geographic analysis, it provides an independent data source to compare with the Parcel File and to validate Parcel File data. The information available from cyclical appraisals is of value to housing and land use planners. For example, many of the housing questions from the 1970 Census, such as value of housing or number of bathrooms, can be answered from the assessment files on a yearly rather than a 10-year basis.

Reports and computer tapes published by the Census Bureau for the decennial census are maintained by Lane Council of Governments and are related to data created locally by the processing programs of the Geographic Data System. Comparisons of the census data with local data can reveal discrepancies. For example, census data indicates the number of dwelling units, by type, for the county, for cities, for each census tract and block. This information can be compared with aggregated data from the Parcel File to determine if a difference exists.

Discovering errors in the census data is important because many revenue allocations are based on census data. Another valuable benefit is the ability to develop statistical relationships between census data, collected infrequently, and local data such as the Parcel File which is updated yearly. By statistical correlations it is possible to estimate other variables, measured only by the census, from trends in the more current local information.

Exhibit A shows the relationship of the information components in the Geographic Data System.

Recent System Development

In 1980, Lane County began to experience a very severe economic slowdown as evidenced by the building permit information shown in Exhibit B. At the same time, the county's share of Federal timber revenues dropped drastically, increasing the pressure on government budgets. Despite this fiscal pressure, RIS has continued to develop and expand. In many situations it is seen as a cost saver and today many government functions are dependent on the system. It has become an operational necessity, not a luxury, that evolved "because top government people trusted each other and were committed (at least in later years) to technology over larger staff."

Unfortunately, public/private cooperation has not always been ideal as discussed in a 1983 Fantus Report: "The community appears to be a collection of disparate interests lacking the ability to merge into large groups capable of broad vision. Instead, a tendency exists to consider issues (including development proposals) along narrow technical or factional lines." As in most communities, a public review process exists which, in the words of an attorney interviewed by Fantus, is "designed to invite opposition." Hence, if a proposal falls short of some group's interests, there is an excellent likelihood that they can squelch it.

The Lane County Geographic Data System plays a critical role in the decision making process by providing data (in a variety of formats) which allows the development community to argue its case from a factual basis, and public

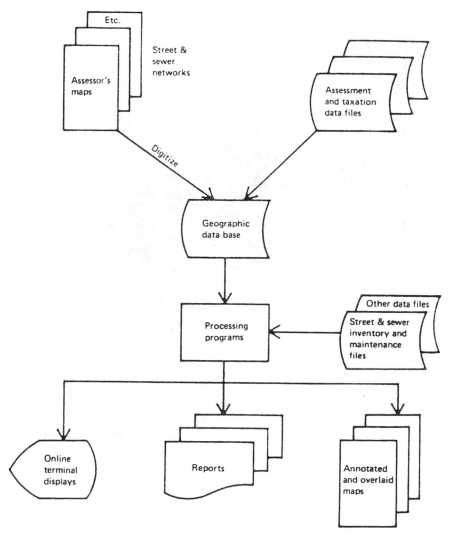

Exhibit A.

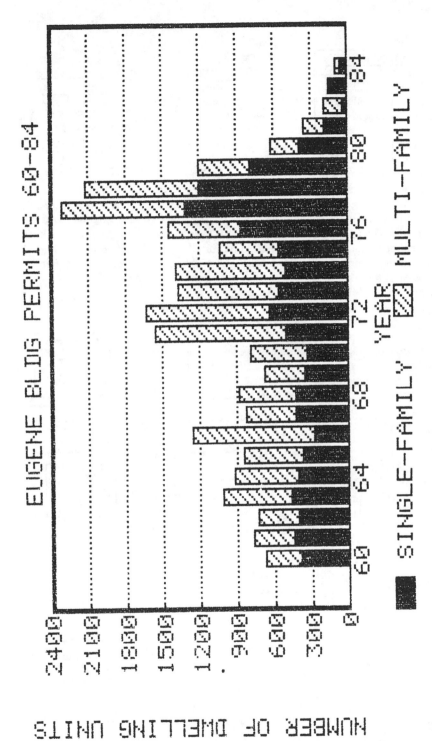

Exhibit B.

decision makers to balance competing positions of various interest groups.

Coupled with continuing slow economic development, this has led to relatively little, given its potential, private sector use of the system. In some ways, Eugene could afford to be laid-back. In the late 1970's, one of five jobs in Lane County, which is the size of Connecticut and has a population of 270,000, was related to the wood-products industry. Unemployment in 1978, as the industry was reaching its peak, was only 5.8% in Eugene. The county treasury was swollen with federal funds—$20 million from the Bureau of Land Management, $15 million from the Forest service, $10 million from other Washington programs. "The money just came in such huge amounts," says Jerry Rust, currently a county commissioner. Then, in 1980, the bubble burst, punctured by 20% interest rates. Dependent as it was on a single industry, Eugene faced the same sort of fate that befell Detroit with cars, Pittsburgh with steel, Akron with rubber. Housing starts dwindled nationally, and demand slumped for the wood used to build them. Men who had made $18 an hour in the nearby forests and mills suddenly were out of work, and unemployment in Lane County jumped to 15% in 1982.

As a final background item, the importance of state level land use planning in Oregon must be mentioned. In 1973, the state began requiring local governments to develop comprehensive plans based on 19 broad goals. While the generality of the goals was meant to reflect compromises between competing statewide interests, the broad definitions stimulated many law suits. One intent of the Statewide Goals is to provide a higher degree of certainty for both the public and private sectors in their decision making processes. Once a land use plan is "acknowledged" as complying with the Statewide Goals, development which is consistent with that plan is difficult to challenge in court. The disadvantage is that the planning process requires a degree of rigor which is unparalleled in most other parts of the country. In complying with the Statewide Planning process, the Eugene-Springfield metropolitan area was able to employ the Geographic Data System to: 1) compare proposed plans with historic trends; 2) develop working materials (including maps); 3) maintain an interactive record of data used to substantiate goal compliance; and 4) maintain a tracking system which allows interactive changes to the comprehensive plan based on changing conditions.

System Elements

The initial geographic data collection began using a small computer on the South Hills Project and was later moved to RIS. The work at RIS began on an IBM 370 facility with each agency responsible for its own programming. The original digitizer was a Calma electromechanical unit.

Today RIS continues to operate a centralized data processing facility on a large IBM mainframe for its six partner agencies. There are over 800 supporting devices, mainly 3270-Type Terminals.

In addition, a complete Synercom Technology Inc. mapping system has recently been installed on a Digital computer (VAX 750) to increase the use and accuracy of geographic information. It is still a parcel specific system and in the city of Eugene all three identifiers are coded for each parcel. Updates come from building permits as well as errors reported by system users. While update time is still a problem, there has been recent progress in conjunction with a major project labeled Common Mapping. The Common Mapping project resulted in the acquisition of the Synercom software system and a new survey to be entered once and be immediately available to multiple agencies without reentry and redrawing of maps.

Specific details on parcel information files and address records are shown in Exhibits C and D, respectively. Present graphics capabilities are described in the "Interactive Graphics Users' Manual" available from the LCOG.

System Use

Government operations are online, but some analytical work is still batch processed. With the exception of the title companies which have been hard-wired into a portion of the system, and use of dial-up access which has recently been added as a system option, all other private sector use is through RIS programmers on a batch processing basis. Collectively, private sector uses are estimated at about 5% of total system's use. Given the system's capabilities, this is at first unexpected. However, given the Oregon land planning process, the traditional rezoning and related infrastructure extension debates, which could involve the utilization of the system, are far less frequent. Furthermore, there are 4,000 fully developed vacant lots and little, if any, activity.

As described in detail in the manuals from which the previously mentioned Exhibits were taken, the system incorporates several data sources and has substantial flexibility both analytically and in output format. All of the assessor's information, tied to address and X-Y coordinate, forms the heart of the system. However, the system is really a collection of related databases with each agency responsible for the compatibility and accuracy of its data.

The entire system is largely an open access operation for government agencies. A notable exception is law enforcement records used in the police dispatch and emergency services operations. Private sector users (other than title companies) make requests to LCOG programmers and do not have direct access to the system.

Since RIS relies on its partner agencies to input data, there is no overall budget. Further, since many people use the system's word processing capabilities one cannot calculate even the hardware and software costs directly attributable to the geographic information system. Utilization of the system is facilitated by mechanically oriented training courses, but there has been little training in the "potential" uses of the system. It is safe to say that the citizens of Eugene like the computer.

Private sector users pay a per hour programmer charge designed to cover marginal cost. Lane County has not thought entrepreneurially about private sector fees. The only marketing is the one brochure shown in Exhibit E.

The main costs "involve convincing people the data is accurate and finding people who know how to use the system. Both are essential for a common dialogue which is one of the chief benefits of the system."

System Problems

The assessor, who is elected, can get behind and this causes the database to at times be "dated". At times the title companies have had to Xerox everything at the courthouse and input it themselves.

Several government agencies must collect a little more data and in a slightly different way than they would if they were just going to use the data internally. The benefits of using other people's information outweigh this cost but it remains an irritant.

The local MLS just implemented a computer system and it is not compatible.

Not all legal information from county records is in the system. Realtors would like more detail on leases. Note: Each state has different property laws so different data is publicly available in different states and consequently system designs will vary accordingly.

Most potential private sector users 1) don't know what data is available; 2) don't know how to access the system; and 3) don't know what questions to ask such a system.

Government cooperation among agencies and departments is not perfect, but is remarkable compared to other areas. For instance: the County Assessor's data is an integral part of the Geographic Data System; there is a common computer system; data is shared among all agencies; there is a multi-agency land use plan—the only one in the state; there are numerous intergovernmental groups which work together to increase governmental efficiencies; L-COG has been one of the most successful councils of government in the country during its 40 years of existence.

Unfortunately the most innovative private developers left Eugene during the economic downturn.

The definition of "developable land" is very difficult because of such uses as "seasonal storage" and "extra parking."

Building permit time is still very long and data doesn't get into the pipeline until the assessor processes a permit. (There is a legal and administrative history by parcel, but that would not be a very useful forecasting tool.)

There is no active consideration by government of downloading or the general idea of a distributive system. The private sector would like to see downloading.

System Improvements

Two years ago, Eugene, Lane County, the Eugene Water and Electric Board, and Lane Council of Governments cooperatively embarked on a "common mapping" project intended to expand the information and productivity

There are three different screen display pages on CLCAP, the HELP page, the PSEUDO TAX LOT page and the TAX LOT display page.

The HELP page gives a short description of the data on CLCAP and instructions on how to access a particular record.

HELP PAGE

*CLCAP: Geographic Data Display   January 1, _____ Data

Map and tax lot:

    _____ _____ ACTION ____   A (ADLIB)   T (TAIMS)   X (CLONE)

Centroid: _____ (X) _____ (Y)   P (CEPLAN) Z (CEZONE) E (EVA)

                                    O (ATSALE)

-------------------------------------- H E L P-I N F O R M A T I O N --------------------------------------

This program accesses the geographic data created by Lane Council of Governments (L-COG). The date in the upper right hand corner indicates the effective date for the data displayed.

PARCEL INFORMATION includes map and tax lot, centroid coordinates, land use, use code and description, number of acres and area (square feet).

ASSESSMENT INFORMATION includes tax levy code, land, improvement and total values, property class, statistical class, year improvement built, and—when applicable—exemption or owner-occupied status.

GEOCODED DATA includes census tract, geo-coded city, zoning, transportation zone, soil type and categories, school district and schools. Also indicated when applicable are urban growth boundary, planned use for the year 2000, and inclusion in the flood plain or greenway.

To request a specific record, enter the map and lot or centroid coordinates in the space provided and press ENTER. After locating a record, you may press ENTER to page to the next record or you may enter a new request.

NOTE: Paging by pressing enter makes sense only when the initial request was by map and lot.

USE ACTION field to access other programs by map and lot.

The TAX LOT display page contains information for a whole tax lot or a land use parcel. This can be determined by the Record type field at the top of the page.

TAX LOT PAGE

*CLCAP: Geographic Data Display   January 1, 1983 Data

Map and tax lot:

    18030511 14000 ACTION: ____   A (ADLIB)   T (TAIMS)   X (CLONE)

Centroid: 1324521 (X) 874538 (Y)   P (CEPLAN) Z (CEZONE) E (EVA)

                                    O (ATSALE)

Record Type: 3 Land use and code: 1111 S SINGLE FAMILY RESIDENTIAL

Number of units: 001

Acres: 0.1158   Area (sqft): 5,044 Old map and lot _____

Exhibit C. *Geographic System data description.*

```
----------------------------------------------- A S S E S S O R' S  D A T A _____.
```
Tax Code   004-00   Property class: 111
Land Value: 16,500   Statistical class: 150
Impr Value: 65,520   Year built: 55
Total Value: 82,020OWNER OCCUPIED PRINCIPAL RESIDENCE
```
--------------------------------------------- G E O C 0 D E D  D A T A --------------------------------------
```
1980 Census Tract: 4900   School District: EUGENE
Block gp/enu 3 dist: 200   Elementary School: 170 EDISON
Year annexed: 1905   Junior hi School: 566 ROOSEVELT
Geo-coded city: EUG   Senior hi School: 660 SOUTH EUGENE
Zoning: R1
Transportation Zone: 197   NEIGHBORHOOD: 11 SOUTH UNIVERSITY
Soil type/cat: 374C / 2000
EUGENE-SPRINGFIELD METRO AREA URBAN GROWTH BOUNDARY
PLANNED USE, 2000: LOW DENSITY RESIDENTIAL

Press ENTER to view next record or type new request.

The PSEUDO TAX LOT display page contains information for parcels which are not actual tax lots but have been assigned fictitious lot numbers for record keeping purposes; such as streets, rivers, railroads, etc. Assessor's and Geocoded Data is not available for pseudo tax lots.

PSEUDO TAX LOT PAGE

*CLCAP: Geographic Data Display   January 1, 1983 Data
Map and tax lot:
     18030511 77 ACTION ___   A (ADLIB)   T (TAIMS)   X (CLONE)
Centroid: 1324137 (X) 874813 (Y)   P (CEPLAN) Z (CEZONE) E (EVA)
                                   O (ATSALE)

Record Type: 3   Land use and code: 4500   Z ROADS AND PARKING
Street name: EMERALD ST
Acres: 1.6495
Area (SQFT): 71,852
Old map and lot: _____
```
-------------------------------- P S E U D O  T A X  L O T  N U M B E R ------------------------------
```
        LOT NUMBER   TYPE OF PARCEL
          00033   Government owned land
          00044   Alley
          00055   Walkway
          00066   Slough/pond/stream
          00077   Road
          00088   River
          00099   Railroad

Exhibit C *(cont.)*

SINGLE FORMAT DISPLAY

SINGLE RECORD DISPLAY (S)

ADDRESS SEQUENCE
NEW FORMAT: ___

NUMBER	DIR	STREET	TYPE	CITY	SEQ

EUG

MAP AND LOT

3170   HARRIS   ST   EUG   76.305 PF

E: 1322371   N: 868913

___ SURVEYED
 X DIGITIZED
___ ESTIMATED

MAP/LOT: 18 03 08 21 10400   LAND USE: 1111   UNITS: 001
ZIP CODE: 97405   CENSUS TRACT: 5000   GEOCODED CITY: EUG

STATUS FLAGS   ___ KEY UPDATE   DATA FLAGS
___ POINTER   ___ DATA UPDATE   ___ NO MAIL
___ OBJECT   ___ ADD
___ XREF   ___ DELETE

Exhibit D. *County-wide address file—User's Manual.*

A New Service—

Computerized Access to
Industrial and Commercially
Zoned Land in
Lane County,
Oregon.

Lane Council of
Governments
Lane County Private
Industry Council
Lane County Employment
and Training Department

Dear Colleague:

In August of 1980, the Lane County Private Industry Council and the Department of Employment and Training provided funds to the Lane Council of Governments to develop a county-wide system for identifying commercially and industrially zoned vacant land. Prior to the completion of this project, such information was available only for the metropolitan area.

L-COG's computerized information on available land makes it now possible to get a printout and/or a map showing all vacant land, by type of zoning, along with the name of the owner, size of parcel, and tax lot number.

We trust you will find this new informational service helpful. To a brighter economic and employment future for all Lane County citizens.

Sincerely,

Steven J. Ickes, Director
Lane County Private Industry Council
Employment & Training Department

Exhibit E.

DEFINITIONS

Undeveloped Land: This term can be defined in several different ways using the available information. First, the land-use code indicates whether the land is **vacant (unused land)**, agricultural (used for agricultural purposes, including orchards, field crops, pasture, or farm) or in timber. Second, the tax assessor's property classification indicates whether the property is considered **vacant for tax purposes**. Third, the improved-value of the tax lot can be used to determine whether the property is undeveloped or nearly so. Each definition has its own use.

Underdeveloped Land: This term can also have several definitions. The file does indicate whether a portion of a tax-lot is undeveloped in the land-use sense. Other definitions can be developed by the user to suit their needs. For example, a lot with a low improved value to land value ratio or low improved value to size ratio might be considered underdeveloped. Similarly, a commercial or industrially zoned parcel with a residential use could be considered underdeveloped. The file provides the flexibility to define the term in the way which best serves the user's needs.

Commercial or Industrial Land: This term includes both lands that are presently zoned commercial or industrial but also those lands having a commercial or industrial plan designation and not so zoned. The second category of lands may require annexation to the city and/or a change in zoning to be developed.

DATA ITEMS!

Map and Lot Number — The Lane County Department of Assessment and Taxation parcel identification number consisting of an eight digit map number followed by a five digit lot number.

Land-use — Lane Council of Governments uses a four digit land use code based on the HUD/BPR standard land use coding system. The code represents the actual use of the land at the date of the file.

Area — The area of each parcel is computed in acres. It can be translated into square-footage.

Exhibit E *(cont.)*

Land-value, Improved-value — These two values are obtained from the Assessment and Taxation files and represent the true cash value as of January 1 of the given year.

Tax-code — Lane County is divided into tax-code areas for the purpose of levying property taxes. The tax-code describes the taxing districts which affect each parcel.

Property-class — This is a three digit code that indicates the classification of property for appraisal purposes. It is similar to zoning. The third digit indicates to the assessor whether the property is vacant, improved, farm land or farm deferred land.

Statistical-class — This is a three digit code that indicates the type of improvement on an improved tax lot. It is similar to, but more general than, the land-use code.

Owner-type — This code indicates publicly owned or other tax exempt property.

City — This code provides the City for each tax lot which is inside corporate limits.

Zoning — This code provides the existing zoning classification for each tax lot. Each jurisdiction has its own zoning ordinance and zoning terminology. It is up to the user to determine the allowed uses and conditions for each zone and jurisdiction.

Urban growth boundary (UGB) — This code indicates whether the tax lot is inside the adopted urban growth boundary of a City. Oregon's Land Conservation and Development Commission (LCDC) requires each city to establish an Urban Growth Boundary to identify and separate urbanizable land from rural land. LCDC must acknowledge each plan and approve the UGB. At this time only Veneta, Dunes City, Westfir and Cottage Grove have acknowledged plans.

Plan Designation — This code indicates the planned use of each tax lot based on the adopted comprehensive plan of each jurisdiction.

Owner's Name and Address — The file has the owner's name and address as indicated by the assessor.

Exhibit E *(cont.)*

Identifying undeveloped commercially and industrially zoned land for Lane County cities is now easier thanks to a **new** computerized listing system developed by Lane Council of Governments (L-COG).

PROMPT AND RELIABLE SERVICE

In no time at all you can receive listings and/or summaries showing all undeveloped land by type of zoning, along with the name and address of the owner, size of parcel and the map and lot number. The same information is also available on computer generated maps.

COMPLETE INFORMATION FOR **ALL** LANE COUNTY CITIES

L-COG, with funding provided by the Lane County Private Industry Council and the Lane County Department of Employment and Training, has updated and extended the Lane County Geographic Data System to include information on commercial and industrial land within the adopted Urban Growth Boundaries of 10 cities outside the Eugene/Springfield Metro area. All of the tax maps have been updated. Existing landuse data and the land area of each parcel was determined. This type of information is now available for 12 cities in Lane County, including the Eugene-Springfield area, as well as: Coburg, Cottage Grove, Creswell, Dunes City, Florence, Junction City, Lowell, Oakridge, Veneta and Westfir.

EASILY ACCESSIBLE AT A REASONABLE PRICE

The L-COG Research Division has **what you need**, located in the Lane County Public Service Building (PSB) at 125 E. 8th Ave. on the Plaza level. Standardized reports have been produced and are obtain-

Exhibit E *(cont.)*

able for **only** the cost of reproduction. Other products can be obtained for a small fee.

Funding for this project was made possible through a grant from the Lane County Private Industry Council and its operational partner the Lane County Department of Employment and Training. This information provides another important component of the PIC's strategy to help stimulate managed economic growth within Lane County.

The system will be maintained and updated on an annual basis by L-COG.

For further information and/or assistance, contact the L-COG Research Division at 687-4283.

Exhibit E *(cont.)*

---

achievements of the Geographic Data System. As part of this process they are upgrading the overall level of the system's geographic data to engineering quality. This is essential if Eugene Water and Electric (an RIS partner) is to use the common data base. With additional software and hardware along with the better survey data, they will have a greatly enhanced mapping capability. Historically, the Lane County system has been information and analysis oriented. Now engineers will be able to use the data and everyone will be able to get enhanced graphics.

They are moving from "home grown" software to vendor software (SAS, Lotus) to improve the likelihood of more frequent updates and more complete documentation.

All of local government now at least talks about making the customer/client number one. This is a critical part of moving to greater private sector usage.

The system is increasingly used in voter registration and canvassing to improve political participation.

Common mapping by speeding the process and improving the graphics will greatly reduce both the public and private need for aerial photography. (Currently the city sells both photos and topos.)

The city phone directory is now on-line as is the municipal code.

The governments have actively increased the use of the system over time. As it becomes integrated into daily operations, it continues to evolve to meet the new needs and improve government service and productivity. The governments are investigating increased private sector access to the system.

Further Information

Publications

Jim Carlson and Jim Croteau, "City of Eugene Land Use Application Record System: CEPLAN," URISA 1984 Conference Proceedings.

City of Eugene, "Status Report–Development Assistance Center," Eugene, Oregon, 1985.

"Eugene, Oregon" IMB Working Paper, 1979.

Lane Council of Governments, "Geographic System Data Description–CLCAP," December, 1983.

Lane Council of Governments, "ADLIB–County Wide Address File Users' Manual," September, 1982.

Lane Council of Governments, "GRAPH–Interactive Graphics Program Users' Manual," March, 1983.

Sheila Mahan, Gary Spivac and Robert Swank, "Plotting Land Use in Oregon," Datamation Magazine, November, 1978.

"Urban Growth Management," Working Paper 35151-338, Lane County, Oregon, 1981.

Clayton Walker and Ed Whitelaw, "Eugene Springfield Real Estate Research Report," Volume III, Fall 1984, Eugene Print, Inc., Eugene Oregon.

Contacts

John Bennett
Lane County Homebuilders
3282 Gateway
Springfield, OR
Phone: (503) 746-2523

Jim Carlson
Program Manager-Research
Lane Council of Governments
125 E. 8th Avenue
Eugene, OR 97401
Phone: (503) 687-4283

Montgomery County Maryland:
Land Data Bank System

Background

A combination of minicomputer and microcomputers is utilized by the Montgomery County Land Data Bank System to maintain an inventory of land parcel information. Also used by its Development Information Management System to monitor subdivision project review information, the computers maintain a current database for the County's extensive planning and development management efforts.

Work on the Land Data Bank System (LDBS) was initiated in 1977 as part of the Planning Board's integrated growth management accounting system, as reported in the "Fourth Annual Growth Policy Report–Carrying Capacity and Adequate Public Facilities." Its first output was published in the 1980 report, "Land Supply and Demand." Prior to 1980, the planning staff had been taking data from the assessor's computerized parcel file with a remote card reader, and then had participated in a bi-county centralized data processing effort. With the addition of a staff computer specialist and a minicomputer, the Planning Board was able to create its own computer land records systems.

The Development Information Management System (DIMS) is a more recent creation. It became operational in 1982. DIMS is used primarily as an office automation tool for administrative purposes, such as generating mailing lists for official notices.

The newest addition to the database is a building permit tracking capability. Upon completion in 1985, it will be able to maintain a rolling, three year history of building permit actions.

All of these systems are operated and maintained by the Research Division of the Montgomery County Planning Board of the Maryland-National Capital Park and Planning Commission. They take data from the tax assessment database, the Washington Suburban Sanitary Commission sewer file, and the building permit file. There is no single collective name by which the systems are known, and their individual names are not known outside the Planning Board, an apparent reflection of their dominant public sector use.

Montgomery County Land Information Systems

System No.	Records	Transactions/Year
LDBS	230,000	27,000
DIMS	4,700	700
Permits	31,000	10,000

The systems are being improved with the creation of linkages between all phases, the addition of several commercial software packages, and the integration of graphic capabilities. Procedures are being developed for improving access by non-governmental users.

System Elements

Hardware and Software. The system hardware includes a Hewlett Packard 3000 minicomputer, a Hewlett Packard 9000 super microcomputer for graphics and modeling, and ten Hewlett Packard 150 microcomputers used as terminals. Another five HP 150's will be in service in 1986. Future plans call for the HP 9000 to be automatically linked to the HP 3000 and to be used for interactive graphics display.

Most of the software was designed in-house. Some commercial packages have been acquired for spreadsheets and graphics for the HP 150's: Visicalc and Lotus 1-2-3. Commercial mapping software is being adapted or acquired for use on the system: Calform for polygon maps on the HP 3000, GIMMS for "incident maps" locating parcels by premise address on the HP 9000, and MSDAMP for plotting patterns in color. Also, GADS 2D is being acquired from Santa Clara County for interactive redistricting for the Board of Education.

Unit of Tabulation. The basic LDBS unit of tabulation is the parcel. Parcel data can be aggregated by a number of geographic subareas.

Parcel Information. Selected parcel information is extracted from the assessor's file, with updates and verification of certain items by the research staff:

District and subdivision
Tax account number
Owners last name
Acres/feet (parcel size)
Acres-feet code
Tax class
Land assessment
Improvement assessment
Taxable land
Taxable improvements
Property class code
Land use code
Assessor's code
Vacant land definition
Zone
Zoning indicator
Stories
Gross floor area
Dwelling units
Census Tract/Block

The Vacant Land definition is assigned to parcels with zero improvement value, farm assessed land, and partially vacant or redevelopable parcels with land value greater than improvement value. The Vacant Land definition excludes public land, all private land having tax exempt status used for cultural and recreational purposes, and other private recreational land such as country clubs and common open space.

Geographic locators are added to the above file by matching the Census Tract/Blocks to a conversion file. Subareas added are: Planning Area, Sewer Category, Traffic Zone, Drainage Basin, and Policy Area.

A third program assigns major land use categories to the file, based on the zoning. Potential dwelling units are calculated based on the effective yield under the applicable zone. During system design, the assessor's 1000 land use codes were simplified and reduced to some 85 land use codes derived from the Standard Land Use Coding Manual and adapted to Montgomery County.

Updates. Updates to the parcel file are entered quarterly. The subdivision file is updated continuously on an interactive basis. Sewer permits are updated quarterly. Building permits will be updated monthly.

System Use

Outputs. Outputs of the land information systems are geared to public decision making purposes. The Land Data Bank System was designed to monitor the supply of residentially zoned land in Montgomery County. The Development Information Management System was designed to track projects in the development pipeline. LDBS is primarily an information system, while DIMS is primarily a management system for tracking both individual subdivisions and the development pipeline. Both are used primarily by the County planners for master planning and growth management, but some private sector use is occurring.

Output formats include printouts, area maps, and summary tables. An example of a regular publication series containing system output is the annual Comprehensive Planning Policies Reports, which include development activity monitoring and thresholds, forecasts for households, population and employment, and development policies and guidelines. (See example table from 1983 Development Report.) Private sector users receive output in printout form.

Pipeline Tracking. Montgomery County regulates its growth in accordance with an adequate public facilities approach, in which the capacities of transportation routes, sewers, and other critical facilities are allocated to policy areas within the County. Each policy area is assigned a "threshold" level of development, balanced with existing and programmed facility capacity. Approved but unbuilt development projects are considered in the development "pipeline". The difference between the threshold and the pipeline equals the number of additional dwelling units that will be permitted in each policy area, until more facilities are added. For example, the chart of Olney Policy Area

Montgomery County Development Report For 1983
(Number of Permits and Actions Processed Between January and December 1983)

	Detached Units	Town-house Units	Apart-ment Units	Total Dwelling Units
Residential				
Sewer Authorizations Issued	1,524	3,197	1,027	5,748
Pre-Preliminary Plans Approved (87 Plans)				
Preliminary Plans Approved (162 Plans)	2,872	4,116	2,615	9,603
Plats Recorded (385 Plats)	2,956	4,138	3,705	10,799
Building Permits Issued	3,951	5,684	1,912	11,547
Completions	2,501	3,313	339	6,133
Commercial and Industrial				
Sewer Authorizations Issued	4.1 million square feet – gross floor area			
Completions	3.2 million square feet – gross floor area			

Development Activity–January-June 1984

	Detached Units	Attached Units	Apart-ment Units	Total Dwelling Units
Residential				
Sewer Authorizations Issued	1,153	882	1,528	3,563
Pre-Preliminary Plans Approved	254			254
Preliminary Plans Approved	5,004		369	5,373
Record Plats Approved	4,947		209	5,166
Building Permits Issued	1,985	2,255	1,530	5,770
Completions	1,521	2,163	1,088	4,772
Commercial and Industrial				
Sewer Authorization Issued	2.6 million square feet – gross floor area			
Preliminary Plans Approved	10			
Record Plats Approved	10			

Source: Montgomery County Planning Board (1985), 1984 Comprehensive Planning Policies Report (Silver Spring: Maryland-National Capital Park and Planning Commission).

data from the 1984 Comprehensive Planning Policies Report (on a following page) shows that 1019 additional dwelling units can be permitted in the Olney Policy Area (the difference between the 5,000 threshold and the 3981 pipeline). Note that both the high and low forecast number of dwelling units are below the pipeline, even in 1995, due to attrition in approved projects which never get completed for various reasons. Of course, the pipeline changes each year as more projects are approved, but decision makers can see potential supply and demand problems at any time period.

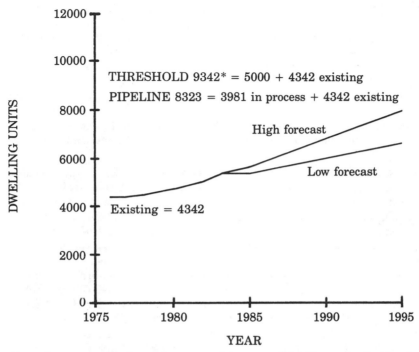

*A total amount of development, expressed in terms of dwelling units, that has been determined by the Planning Board to be balanced appropriately, on the basis of an area wide average, with the existing and programmed facilities for the area.

Olney Policy Area dwelling units. (Source: Montgomery County Planning Board (1985), 1984 Comprehensive Planning Policies Report [Silver Spring: Maryland-National Capital Park and Planning Commission].)

DIMS monitors each project in the pipeline through the required steps: preliminary plat approval, sewer allocation review, record plat approval and recording, sewer permit granting, building permit granting, and completion of construction and occupancy permit. It is used to manage the administrative process. DIMS has interactive query routines in which users can call up plans (pre-preliminary, preliminary, record plat, or site plan), subdivision data, and land use data by time periods, geographic areas, and other parameters.

Data Sources. The assessor's tape is a major source of parcel information. It is supplemented with information from building permit applications, sewer authorizations, subdivision requests, zoning applications, and housing completions. Parcels are tracked through the files by their tax account numbers.

Users and Uses. In addition to various divisions of the Planning Board, governmental users of the systems include the Washington Suburban Sanitary Commission which seeks holding capacity data based on vacant land, the

County Council which seeks information for sending notices on plan and zoning changes, the Housing Opportunities Commission which seeks information on potential public housing areas, the Department of Economic Development which uses the inventory of vacant industrial property, the Board of Education which uses the subdivision file, and various other County, local and regional agencies.

Realtors and appraisers have been the primary private sector users of the land supply information in the system. Some private development consultants are beginning to realize the value of system information. Private sector users are charged fifty cents per page of printout to recover the costs of the system.

Access. Despite the fact that the systems are not marketed, the Research Division receives five to six requests for data per day. A user asking for the location of vacant parcels in a particular planning district with a certain type of zoning can get a printout within a week. He would also have to refer to the assessor's tax maps, though when computer mapping is completed he could get them from the Research Division. If private sector requests continue to increase, a full time staff person may be needed to handle them.

Several private computerized land information services are available in Montgomery County. The Sager microfiche system, LUSKNET–a new online real estate information system, the Montgomery County Board of Realtors computerized Multiple Listing Service, and the Moholt Data Service listing comparable sales information are among the current private services. Most of these make use of County data, but also offer additional information, custom formats, more frequent reporting, and other features.

System Problems

Initial problems with data accuracy hampered development of the Land Data Bank System. The tax assessor's Parcel File contained errors in the assignment of zoning codes and Census Tract Blocks, which required considerable verification and correction effort. Mistakes also occurred during the transformation of assessment records to include planning data, especially in listing the map reference numbers and premise addresses. Questions remain about the accuracy of some fields on the parcel file, as on the subdivision file.

Montgomery County has not done much to make its information widely accessible or useful to private sector users. Current users tend to be data analysis experts, who have discovered that there is a wealth of information available if they can extract it. Many of them rely on personal contacts with individual County staff. They must choose between two land databases. The Planning Board uses the assessor's database; Economic Development uses a different database. Because Montgomery County land data is not published in regular reports, users must construct their own report formats and trend indicators. The tax assessor will not permit modem access. Users can buy copies of the assessor's computer tape but must copy current data from microfiche, incurring high time costs. The County has not marketed its land supply data to private users or arranged for it to be available at an information counter.

More timely information would be more useful. This could aid the private market in avoiding roller coaster swings of oversupply of developed space.

System Improvements

During 1985, the parcel and subdivision files will be integrated as a linked system. Along with the new building permit data, this will enable them to strengthen policy maker capabilities to track the pipeline.

A contemplated major improvement to the system involves the addition of parcel and project mapping integrated with the data files. A pilot project on this is underway.

Another improvement in process is aimed at improving user access through menu-driven programs at user terminals. This is not an immediate prospect for implementation.

Further Information

Publications.
Montgomery County Planning Board (1985) 1984 *Comprehensive Planning Policies Report.* Silver Spring, MD: Maryland-National Capital Park and Planning Commission.

———(1980) *Land Supply and Demand.* Silver Spring, MD: Maryland-National Capital Park and Planning Commission.

Contacts
Drew Dedrick
Chief of Research Division
Montgomery County Planning Board
8787 Georgia Avenue
Silver Spring, MD 20907
Telephone: (301) 495-4700

Robert L. Rudnick
Supervisor of Assessments
51 Monroe Street, Suite 400
Rockville, MD 20850
Telephone: (301) 279-1431

Richard Tustian
Planning Director
Montgomery County Planning Board
8787 Georgia Avenue
Silver Spring, MD 20907
Telephone: (301) 495-4500.

New Haven, Connecticut
Land Use Information System (LUIS)

Background

LUIS is a microcomputer based information system which contains records from numerous New Haven city departments on individual land parcels. The system began operation in 1984, although its roots go back to the 1970's. LUIS is operated by the Office of Housing and Neighborhood Development rather than by the Planning Department, and this is a distinguishing characteristic of both the functioning and the use of the system. The principal goals of LUIS are not in monitoring development, as New Haven is not a growing city, but in providing information on and analysis of, the housing stock, neighborhood change, and land use. It has already been used for an Abandoned House Program, Neighborhood Commercial Areas Revitalization, the Weatherization Program and a Tax Foreclosure/Tax Abatement Program.

History of LUIS. New Haven has been building its experience with micro computers to aid in program analysis for a number of years. Late in the 1970's, an attempt was made to create an arson early warning and prevention system, AWAPS, which permitted users to query four independent city files through a remote terminal. The user could view on-screen a parcel's basic description, plus its recent history of fires, non-payment of taxes, liens, and code violations. For a time, this was extremely useful, but AWAPS soon showed its limitations. The parcel database was too limited, there was an inability to group and display various types of parcels, and no statistical analysis could be performed. The data became obsolete quickly because no provision was made for regular updating of the files by the various departments.

The impetus for LUIS goes back to efforts to create a database on neighborhood change. It was further stimulated in 1983, when New Haven joined the Connecticut Housing Finance Authority in a $20 million program to finance the rehabilitation of vacant buildings. A comprehensive information system was necessary for this program in order to document the extent of the problem (about 2 percent of the city's residential structures were vacant in 1981), to manage the program effectively and to respond to housing circumstances. The new computer system was able to track the rehabilitation process on each building, prepare lists of available properties, and perform analyses of the housing stock.

Work on the new system was begun in the Fall of 1983, and it became operational in August, 1984. The costs of setting up the system were as follows:

Development Costs

Hardware and Software	$ 40,000
Programmer/Analysts	43,000
Outside Consultants	23,000
Miscellaneous	12,000
Total	$118,000

LUIS in Relation to Other Municipal Information. New Haven's tax assessor records have been computerized for over 10 years. The city has a mainframe computer which could have been used to build the land use information system. The Office of Housing and Neighborhood Development (OHND) decided instead to acquire a microcomputer large enough to store the complete land parcel file and to maintain this system independently of the city's data processing department. OHND's reason for this decision can perhaps be understood from a statement made about the experience of other cities with mainframes in a OHND draft report on LUIS:

They [mainframes] are often understaffed, poorly understood, or operated by programmers far removed from many of the actual purposes and priorities underlying new requests for data processing. As a result, policy-makers and administrators needing information quickly came to distrust the data processing operations center. Instead of joining together to create a commonly shared data base, agency heads still dispatched and used their own personnel where possible.

LUIS is operated by OHND, receiving data input from the assessor's data tapes and from other operating departments as detailed below. It is a separate information system, although cooperation between departments is excellent.

Planned Development of the System. New sources of information are added to the parcel records periodically. Census data by tract can be used in conjunction with city information to produce profiles of neighborhoods or census tracts. The city plans to increase the access to LUIS by the addition of new micros and terminals. Currently, all but one terminal for the use of the system are located in OHND. Private sector access is planned also, although no specific facilities for this use have been proposed. The private sector use of the system at present operates by having requests for information cleared by the director of OHND and then passed on to the operational head, who delivers the information to the individual making the request.

The experience of using LUIS to analyze land use data has called attention to problems with some of the ways in which land use has been classified in New Haven. In order to standardize the land use classification system and to establish a unique street address for each land parcel in the city (currently many vacant parcels do not have addresses), the Sanborn Map Company has been engaged to correct the existing parcel maps during the Summer of 1985.

New Haven does not plan to make any major changes to LUIS beyond the improvements outlined above. The microcomputer now in use is not large enough for efficient digitized parcel mapping, so that the main changes which can be made within the current framework are the addition of new data files.

System Elements

Hardware. Mainframe and minicomputers were eliminated from consideration because of their acquisition and site preparation cost and their staffing requirements. Personal computers were also not feasible because they are limited to a single user and because of the lack of available statistical and database management packages.

The original system chosen was a super microcomputer, the Altos S586-40. The basic system came with 512k bytes of random access memory, a twenty-megabyte hard disk unit, and one 1.2 megabyte floppy disk drive. New Haven also purchased a forty-megabyte hard disk drive. The system could accommodate five terminals; four of these were located at OHND and the last was at the Office of Building Inspection. Detailed specifications of this original system can be found in the Appendix to this case study. In mid-1985 New Haven upgraded their hardware to an Altos 986, which can accommodate nine terminals.

The department also owns several Radio Shack TRS-80 microcomputers. The TRS-80 is needed for statistical analysis of the data and for producing maps and graphs. This is discussed more fully in the software section below. OHND also plans to acquire an IBM-XT, which will be hardwired to the present system for expansion.

Software. The operating system chosen for the Altos is XENIX, developed by Microsoft from Bell Lab's UNIX operating system. XENIX is reputed to be the best system currently available for microcomputers, and as it is very widely used it promises to be the standard for the industry in the future if any system is to achieve that status. XENIX is a powerful multiuser system with a number of valuable data manipulation utilities and text editors. Using XENIX, it is relatively easy to port in existing application software from other existing microcomputers under XENIX.

In choosing a database management system for use with XENIX, OHND was most concerned with the following characteristics: multiuser capabilities, storage capacity (26,000 parcel records for the city plus over 7000 blockface records), power and flexibility of data retrieval, ease with which data could be imported and exported to and from other software and hardware systems, and, finally, general ease of use.

The package which was chosen to fill these requirements was Unify Corporation's Unify Database Management System. This package was designed to be a multiuser system. It has a powerful report writer feature, a "screen paint" screen development facility, a user controlled help facility, a powerful retrieval and update language and very good data import and export capabilities. The version used is release 3.1, which became available in August, 1984.

Although Unify permits the user to perform a variety of statistical techniques, it does not have mapping capability. When more sophisticated analyses are appropriate, data can be transferred to the TRS-80, where statistical analysis is possible using the SOLIR software package. SOLIR can also produce digitized maps at the Census Tract level.

SOLIR, or Small On-Line Research, was developed by the Lincoln Land Institute for use by municipal governments' property assessors. It is available free of charge to any jurisdiction which sends a representative to a one-week training course. The system contains the various software elements that permit one to design databases, enter and maintain the data and perform various statistical and other computational activities. It also permits the user to display the results on a computer screen, printer, or plotter, estimate property values and transfer data between computers. Data is stored on eight-inch floppy disks, each with the capacity to hold up to 125 pieces of information on 1500 records (in this case, each record is a land parcel). A hard disk system is available to expand the capacity to 30,000 records. SOLIR is attractive because of its storage capacity, flexibility and low cost (a complete system including hardware and software can be acquired for about $16,000).

Unit of Tabulation. LUIS is based on individual land parcels. Each record contained information on one of the 26,000 parcels in the city of New Haven. Parcels are identified from the city assessor's master file, and each is coded with its street address and the unique map block parcel number from the assessor's parcel maps.

Parcel Information. The parcel information contained in LUIS is assembled from a variety of sources. Each record contains, besides the address and assessor's identifying number, the name of the property's owner, the assessed value, a land use code, and information on taxes, fires since 1980, housing code violations, building permits, property transfers, mortgages and background Census data. Parcels can be accessed by owner's name, street address or assessor's number. Figure 1 presents an example of the display which is provided when a property is called up. Figure 2 is the pre-formatted display for property transfers, and Figure 3 is the vacant building format. Census tract information from the 1980 census is stored in SOLIR on the TRS-80. Files from the Altos must be transferred to the TRS in order to produce reports which use combined census and parcel information. Parcel information is described in more detail below under "Data Sources."

At present LUIS is installed on the Altos as a single database application consisting of four record types:

1. The basic parcel record type – 26,000 parcels
2. The geobase record type – 7200 records (one per city blockface)
3. A property transfer record type – one record per transfer of property (expands over time)
4. A building permit record type – about 4000 building permit records going back to 1980.

Updates. Basic information that changes infrequently is updated on an annual basis. This is mainly the Assessor's Grand List, which comprises the foundation of the information system. Other blocks of information, such as the record of back taxes due and the list of fire and health emergency calls, are revised every six months. Changes in property ownership are among the most important data in the system and need to be as up-to-date as possible. These

SCREEN FORMATTER

SCREEN LAYOUT

parorof1

```
0:                                                                          :0

1:   SCREEN LAYOUT                                                          :1

2:   parorof1                                                              :2

3:                                                                          :3

4:  | Map/Blk/Parcel: x     Address: x   x   NSA: x   Neighbrhd: x   To: x  :4

5:  | Census Tract: x       Blockface: x                            Ward: x :5

6:                                                                          :6

7:  Zoning: x    Variances: x     Landuse: x    Multiple Use: x  No. Cds: x :7

8:  Class Code: *x*   Ownership: x   Acq dat: x    Sale Date: x    Type: x  :8

9:  Sale Price: x     Sale Code: x     No. of Living Units: **x       ***   :9

10: -----OWNERSHIP----                                                     :10

11:  Name: x                     Name2: x                                  :11

12:  | Addr. x                                                             :12

13:  | Addr. x                                                             :13

14:                                         Side of Street: x              :14

15:  Frontage: x    Depth: x     Area: x               Land Value: $x      :15

16:  VDO Code: x    Liv.Units: x   Built: lx   Rooms : x   Bldg. Value: $x :16

17:  Stories: x   Style: x   Walls x   Condition: x      OutBld. Val: $x   :17

18:  1977 Pre-Reassessment Assessed Value: $x        78 Mkt               :18

19:  x   #:x   Susp: x   w/Dam: x    Totdam: $x   Strfired x   StrDam: $x  :19

20:  Earliest Btax yr: 'x   No. Yrs: x   Last Paymt :x   Btax Balance : $x :20

21:                                                                        :21

22:                                                                        :22

23:                                                                        :23
```

Figure 1. Uses for inquiries and data. (Source: *New Haven Office of Housing and Neighborhood Development, Managing Municipal Information Needs Using Micro-Computers: Conference Summary and Background Materials*, October 4-5, 1984.)

SCREEN FORMATTER
SCREEN LAYOUT
transfer

```
 0:
 1:
 2:
 3:
 4:              ****PROPERTY TRANSFERS****
 5:
 6:  Address         :x            High St. No.:  x
 7:
 8:  Condominium No. : x           Map/Blk/Parcl : x
 9:
10:  Grantor    : x
11:
12:  Grantee    : x
13:  Grantee Addr1 : x             Addr2:  x
14:
15:  Date    : x     Deed: x       Instrument No.  x
16:
17:  Sales Price   : x    Primary Mortgage: x    Lender:  x
18:  Interest Rate : x
19:
20:
21:
22:
23:
```

Figure 2. *Property transfer profile. (Source: New Haven Office of Housing and Neighborhood Development, Managing Municipal Information Needs Using Micro-Computers: Conference Summary and Background Materials, October 4-5, 1984.)*

```
                         SCREEN FORMATTER
                         SCREEN LAYOUT
                            vachlog
0:
1:
2:
3:  Record No: x                          Map/Block/Parcel: x
4:  Addr: x to x = x        Tract: x    Nbd: x    File Opened: x
5:  Owner: x                                            Revised: x
6:  Owner Add: x                                        Acquired: x
7:
8:  Description: x                  Lien Amt: $ x    DU: x
9:  Lot Size: x      x             Code Viol:        Class Code: x
10: Hist Desig:   Date Built: 1x   Fires: x :  x   Rooms: x      Photo: x
11: Market Value: $ x                              Since: x      Date: x
12: Rehab Cost: $ x   Acquis Cost: $ x   Tax Arrearage: $ x
13: Inspector: x      Seller: x      Future Value: $ x   Appraiser: x   Date: x
14: Condition: x                       Source: x     Date: x
15: Programs 1: x      2: x      3: x
16: Comments: x                        Source: x     Date: x
17: 01 IND Rec: x: x   ABC Rec 1: x Date: x   Rec 2: x   Date: x
18:      Status 1: x : x   Date: x     Source: x     Date: x
19:      Status 2: x  x                Source: x     Date: x
20:
21:
22:
23:
```

Figure 3. *Vacant building profile. (Source: New Haven Office of Housing and Neighborhood Development, Managing Municipal Information Needs: New Haven's Experience with Micro-Computers, Draft Report, September 1984.)*

are revised every two weeks by OHND staff. Updating practices are summarized in the table below:

Information Updating Frequency

Information	Yearly	Biannually	Monthly	Biweekly
Assessor's grand List	x			
Tax delinquencies		x		
Fires		x		
Code violations			x	
Building permits			x	
Property transfers				x
Census data—every 10 years				

System Use

Outputs. The output of LUIS is designed to provide a variety of profiles and analyses of neighborhood trends, ownership changes, building condition and other information for OHND and other departments in city government as well as, to a lesser degree, to individuals and institutions outside of government. The simplest profile is the property description shown in Figure 1. These profiles are the most frequent request for information from the system, usually with respect to a single property.

Other requests for information often deal with ownership of property, lists of properties in a particular vicinity, mortgage lending activity, building permits and neighborhood information. There are two pre-formatted reports produced from the system (see Figure 4); one is a weekly listing of property transfers which have occurred, and the other is a list of abandoned buildings with addresses and back taxes, for purposes of selling them to be rehabilitated.

As shown in Figure 4, the system is also used to study neighborhood characteristics as an input to policy discussions and program design. Digitized maps can be produced to display housing and economic characteristics by census tract, using both municipal data and census information.

Vacant and Developable Land. New Haven is not a growing city, and there are no large amounts of undeveloped land within its boundaries. Development is of the infill variety; consequently, the land information system focuses on changes in land use and vacant parcels rather than on the supply of raw land for development. Parcels are identified as vacant, but there is no further breakdown into categories of development potential. A private sector user of the system who wished to identify available parcels would be able to check the zoning on a vacant parcel, its current owner, the last transfer of the property which occurred, and other public information in the file. There is also no indication of the physical characteristics of a parcel to help gauge its development potential. The only plans OHND has in this area are to include wetlands

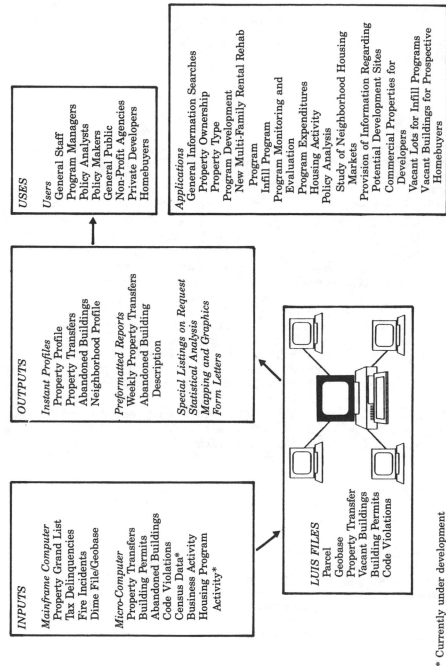

INPUTS

Mainframe Computer
Property Grand List
Tax Delinquencies
Fire Incidents
Dime File/Geobase

Micro-Computer
Property Transfers
Building Permits
Abandoned Buildings
Code Violations
Census Data*
Business Activity
Housing Program
    Activity*

LUIS FILES
Parcel
Geobase
Property Transfer
Vacant Buildings
Building Permits
Code Violations

OUTPUTS

Instant Profiles
Property Profile
Property Transfers
Abandoned Buildings
Neighborhood Profile

Preformatted Reports
Weekly Property Transfers
Abandoned Building
    Description

Special Listings on Request
Statistical Analysis
Mapping and Graphics
Form Letters

USES

Users
General Staff
Program Managers
Policy Analysts
Policy Makers
General Public
Non-Profit Agencies
Private Developers
Homebuyers

Applications
General Information Searches
Property Ownership
Property Type
Program Development
New Multi-Family Rental Rehab
    Program
Infill Program
Program Monitoring and
    Evaluation
Program Expenditures
Housing Activity
Policy Analysis
Study of Neighborhood Housing
    Markets
Provision of Information Regarding
    Potential Development Sites
Commercial Properties for
    Developers
Vacant Lots for Infill Programs
Vacant Buildings for Prospective
    Homebuyers

* Currently under development

Figure 4. *Diagram of the Land Use Information System.* (Source: *New Haven Office of Housing and Neighborhood Development, Managing Municipal Information Needs Using Micro Computers: Conference Summary and Background Materials,*" *October 4-5, 1984.*)

and other topographical data using the census geo-coding system. Of course, this would be by Census Tract and not by land parcel.

Data Sources. The information assembled for LUIS comes from a variety of city government sources, from the federal census and from private sources. Thus it is an integration of already-existing data. For the most part, this data is collected twice; that is, the Office of Building Inspection collects its information and records it in its own files, then inputs it also into LUIS. This duplication does not really apply to the largest part of LUIS, however, because the assessor's records are already on a mainframe computer, so that the only additional work involved for LUIS is to read data from the assessor's tape into the Altos system.

The basic building block of the system is the property information obtained from the Assessor's Grand List; this includes such items as owner name and address, number of dwelling units, and assessed value. As mentioned before, this data is on computer tape and is copied for use by OHND. Data on tax delinquencies and fires come from the Tax Collector's Office and the Fire Department, respectively. These data are also on computer tape maintained by the Data Processing Center.

Information which must be updated more frequently is entered directly by OHND staff or by staff members of the departments providing the data. Building permits. property transfers and mortgages are obtained and entered by OHND staff. The Office of Building Inspection and Enforcement has the only terminal connected to LUIS outside OHND, and Building Inspection enters the code violations data themselves. This department was included in the design of LUIS because both OHND and Building Inspection could benefit from the use of the system. In this process, Building Inspection was able to include information in LUIS which they could use, and this made their participation in maintaining the system much more willing.

Property transfers are a crucial piece of information in the system, and one which must be as timely as possible. Because of the long time lag in obtaining this information from the Assessor's Grand File, OHND uses the Commercial Record as its source for transfers. This will be discussed more fully below under "System Problems."

Users. The principal users of the system are:

- The Office of Housing and Neighborhood Development
- The Office of Building Inspection and Enforcement
- The Development Administrator
- Other City Departments
- Neighborhood Groups
- The Real Estate Industry.

Uses

Vacant Building Rehabilitation Program. LUIS has been invaluable in documenting the location and number of vacant buildings and in monitoring the purchase and rehab of these structures by individuals. This program is at the core of New Haven's push to strengthen their neighborhoods' economic base and create stability. Several officials stated that this program alone made LUIS worthwhile.

LUIS makes it possible to produce up-to-date lists of vacant buildings on a weekly basis. This list is provided to realtors and individuals who are interested in purchasing them. OHND can also monitor the progress of a rehab by keeping track of the process from purchase through issuance of a building permit to the occupancy or sale of the property and its re-entry on the tax rolls.

Infill Program. New Haven is also interested in promoting economic development through the construction of residential units on vacant land within the city. The use of LUIS allows them to estimate the impact of development in terms of tax effects and economic benefits to the neighborhood.

Analysis of Housing and Neighborhood Activity. OHND uses LUIS to produce comprehensive data on neighborhood change and economic activity. They are interested in changes in ownership patterns and in mortgage lending activity. Economic trends can be used to demonstrate to lenders the positive change in an area which warrants greater lending. The director of OHND emphasizes that LUIS is used to design, not merely to monitor, programs. Knowledge of neighborhoods allows policy-makers to target aid programs and other initiatives to areas where they will be most effective.

Building Conditions. The Office of Building Inspection uses LUIS to monitor the patterns of code violations and tax delinquencies to be better informed of problem areas and to act more quickly than they could before. Since the Arson Warning and Prevention tapes have been merged with the system, this information can also be used to pinpoint problem areas in the city.

Private Sector Users. To date, there has been very little private sector use of the system. Residential development is normally on a single parcel basis and does not require any information from LUIS. A few commercial developers have made requests for information, hut this has been mostly for data on a few parcels. There have been no large printouts or analyses as such done for the private sector.

The main benefit of the system for the private sector has been of an indirect kind. OHND produces lists of abandoned buildings each week and provides them to realtors who market them to individuals. The realtors have been enthusiastic about this service, and the local real estate board has suggested further cooperation by jointly recording housing sales which go into the system and into the Multiple Listing Service. While OHND is interested in this idea, no action has been taken as yet.

Budget. The annual operating cost of LUIS has been estimated as follows:

Staff	$42,000
Programmer/Analyst	25,000
Miscellaneous	5,000
Total	$72,000

This does not include any additions to the hardware or software, for which no definite plans exist.

Access. At present there is no time-sharing access to the system by private users. As stated above, all but one of the terminals for the Altos microcomputer are housed at OHND. If a private user desires information, a request must be submitted to the director of OHND. This is approved by the director and passed on to the staff, who provide the information.

OHND foresees greater private sector use of the system in the future. At present there are no plans to allow online access by outside users. However, the recent upgrade of system hardware to an Altos 986 with nine terminals has expanded the capacity for internal use. An IBM PC or XT can now be used as a remote terminal, and the larger number of terminals has allowed OHND to add additional files and to develop the system while maintaining the level of use by city departments.

Pipeline Tracking. Since there is no undeveloped land in New Haven to be developed, LUIS does not track the development process for residential construction. The system was established to deal with the abandoned building problem, and in this area some tracking is done. The stock of abandoned buildings is monitored, the number of sales, building permits issued, and the date at which these buildings go back on the tax rolls are tracked.

Vacant land is also included in the system, so that it is possible to measure the amount of land zoned a particular way which is available. And since building permits are also collected, this stage of the development process can be seen. However, there is no information on construction awards, stage of the construction process or other measures of development activity.

Private Sector Information System Relationships. At present there are no private sector information systems which interact with LUIS. As mentioned above, there has been some discussion of merging the Multiple Listing Service data with the system, but there are no plans at present to do this. The Sanborn Map Company, which was engaged to re-map the city during the Summer of 1985, has been enthusiastic about LUIS and has mentioned the possibility of using the system for commercial purposes.

System Problems

The problem which has consumed the most time for the OHND staff is the accurate listing of property addresses. The assessor's identifying number is unique for each parcel, but the users of the system most often want to search a property by street address. The staff found that many street addresses were missing, inaccurate or not unique (two or more streets with the same name, etc.). Many vacant lots did not have addresses. This has been dealt with by correcting addresses as the users encounter problems. It is also one of the main reasons for using Sanborn Map Company to check all addresses. Since users of LUIS often cannot find a property they are looking for when the address is entered, OHND maintains a hard copy listing of all properties by street address. They have found that users can often find what they are looking for by scanning the listing for the street on which the wanted property is located.

The other problem which was mentioned in interviews deals with the time lag in obtaining the recent property transfer information. There is a two-month lag in the reporting of transfers from the deeds office to the assessor's office. Then a three-month lag occurs before the transfers are available on the assessor's tape. To avoid these delays, OHND has been using the privately-produced Commercial Record, which has about a three-week lag between the actual transfer and the publication of the Record. The assessor's office is working to eliminate the three-month lag at their end, but this would still make the Record more timely than the assessor. The assessor stated that the Record was only about 90 percent accurate, so that there would be a benefit to using the official records if they could be made available more quickly. An ideal system would be for the property transfers to be entered into a computer system as they are recorded, with access by both the Commercial Record and the assessor or OHND on-line.

System Improvements

Most of the changes which will occur in LUIS for the near term are evolutionary improvements. More data files will be entered, and existing files will be improved for accuracy. OHND plans to acquire an IBM-XT to expand the system's core capacity and to add more terminals. Additional departments may be given terminals.

There is also an effort being made to make full use of the system's ability to analyze neighborhood data as an input to policy-making. More economic information and business activity information will be added, so that trends can be seen in downtown and neighborhood development. This is seen as a tool for documenting the changes taking place in various parts of the city. OHND's interest is in convincing mortgage lenders to increase their lending in particular areas by showing them evidence of positive economic trends. The focus in the past has been on residential activity, but policy-makers are thinking increasingly of the need to look at downtown commercial development. The harbor is currently undergoing development, and the city is looking for ways to use LUIS to aid in this effort also.

Further Information

Publications. The two reports from which much of the material in this case study has been drawn are:

"Pilot Neighborhood Analysis: Using SOLIR Software Package," Office of Housing and Neighborhood Development, November 1983.
"Managing Municipal Information Needs: New Haven's Experience with Micro-Computers," OHND, September 1984.

In addition, OHND is preparing a manual on the use of LUIS to be available by the Fall of 1985.

Contacts. For information regarding the operation of LUIS, contact

Daniel Kops, Coordinator, Information System Development
Office of Housing and Neighborhood Development
157 Church St.
New Haven, CT 06510
(203) 787-7090

For information on the use of LUIS in policy analysis, contact

Gerardo Canto, Director
Office of Housing and Neighborhood Development
157 Church St.
New Haven, CT 06510
(203) 787-8378

Appendix: Altos S5B6-40 Hardware Specifications

Processor:
Altos 586-40

- 16-bit processor operating at 10 MHz
- 6 serial ports, supporting from one to five concurrent users plus a printer
- 512Kb RAM memory

Disk Storage:
One floppy disk drive – 1Mb capacity 5¼" diskettes
One forty megabyte hard disk
(System capacity =2 40Mb drives)

Printer:
  Okidata microline 84

CRT Terminals:
  One Altos II terminal
  Four Wyse 50 terminals

Current hardware list prices:
  Altos 586-40 with 40 Mb hard disk,
One 1Mb floppy disk,
One Altos III crt terminal,
and the Xenix runtime system $9,900.
Okidata Printer (approximate) $1,200.
Wyse 50 terminals (approximate per term) $ 600.

San Diego, California:
Urban Information System (UIS)

Background

The city of San Diego's Urban Information System (UIS) was developed over several years in the early 1970's. The on-line permit tracking module of UIS was incorporated into the system in 1975. UIS was originally developed in order to provide management with estimates of future impacts of growth so that public facility decisions could be made which were in line with growth trends. The need for an integrated monitoring system increased when the city enacted a three-tiered growth management program in the late 1970's. This program classified the city into urbanized areas, planned urbanizing areas, and future urbanizing areas, and restricted the amount of land available for development. UIS was needed in order to document whether or not there was enough unrestricted land available for projected growth through 1995.

The city departments which initiated UIS were the Data Processing Corporation (a non-profit entity formerly a part of city government) and the Planning Department. Other departments collaborating in the design of the system included the Engineering and Development Department and the Building Department. UIS is an IBM mainframe-based system, with interactive mainframe software used. Computer programs were mainly designed in-house by personnel in the Data Processing Corporation (DPC). In addition to DPC doing data processing tasks and maintaining the computer programs, city departments involved in entering data into UIS include Planning, Engineering and Development, and Building.

UIS is but one of several land-related automated systems in the city. Most other automated systems are mainframe or minicomputer oriented and are operated on the IBM mainframe computers of DPC. A few of these automated systems are:

- Street Address Network (geographic identification system),
- AIRS (a system in support of building permit processing and building inspections scheduling),
- Facilities financing system operated by the Engineering and Development Department,
- Three systems operated by the fire department for reporting of fire incidents and scheduling of inspections,
- CORPIS (operated by the Property Department for managing information about City owned property),
- Automated Regional Justice Information System (ARJIS) is operated by a joint powers agency with data processing services provided by the San Diego Data Processing Corporation. All of the police agencies in the region participate in ARJIS, which includes geographic analysis capabilities as well as other crime prevention, case tracking and investigatory tools.

- Land Use Information System (LUIS) is used by Planning to extract and reformat land use information from the current Assessment Roll.

Two important automated systems outside city government are:

- San Diego Area Governments (SANDAG) operates a geographic information system on minicomputer with a variety of graphic and nongraphic peripherals,
- San Diego Gas & Electric has implemented a county-wide automated facilities mapping program. This IBM mainframe-based system is a computer drafting system linked to a database for the facilities and parcel information.

In May of 1984, the City and County of San Diego signed an agreement for the development of a Regional Urban Information System (RUIS). Tasks outlined in the scope of work include: expansion of the area of coverage to all parcels in unincorporated San Diego County, modifying certain parts of existing systems so as to allow the county to use the existing data processing capabilities in the city's UIS, and accomplishing a new and enhanced design for a land-based regional system (forecasted to contain close to 1 million parcels).

System Elements of UIS

Hardware. UIS is a centralized data processing system, with terminals in the user departments having on-line access to the IBM 3031 mainframes in DPC. Minicomputers and microcomputers are used in other departments (such as Fire and Police), but are not part of UIS.

Software. Software is predominantly in-house computer programs written mainly in COBAL language. The database is hierarchical in nature (grandfather-father-son structure). The interactive mainframe software is largely menu-driven, presenting the user with a choice of options at selected decision points in the program. Computer programs are written to provide on-line access to the UIS database. There is presently no computer mapping capability as part of UIS, although a polygon-based mapping system is scheduled to be part of RUIS.

SAS is also extensively used for analysis, graphics and reporting of data. The local SAS installation, operating in a TSO (Time Sharing Option) environment, provides users throughout the City with easy interactive tools for handling automated data. The staff of San Diego Data Processing Corporation have developed front-end panels which allow relatively unsophisticated users to develop databases and analysis procedures on their own. Business chart and graph capabilities are provided as well as spreadsheet and statistical analysis tools. With the assistance of programmer/analysts, almost any data contained in files and databases maintained on City computers may be loaded into SAS for use by professional staff. This avoids the need to develop many specific, single-use programs by permitting ad hoc analysis tailored to the current demand.

Another tool being introduced into the data processing environment is a query language (ASI/INQUIRY, Applications Software, Inc.) which allows direct access to databases without intervention of programmer/analysts. This interactive tool will make it even less necessary to develop standard report programs for specialized use.

Major components of UIS include:

- Development Monitoring System (DMS) - tracks permit actions
- Land Use Inventory (LUIS) - parcel based information used for summarization of land use trends
- Site Profile - provides detailed parcel-specific information, with multiple access points
- UIS also interfaces with systems such as Street Address Network and the building permit systems (AIRS).

Unit of Tabulation. The basic building block for UIS is the tax parcel, as defined by the County Assessor's office. There are roughly one-third of a million parcels in the City system. The most frequently used levels of aggregation are the census tract and community planning area, of which there are approximately 50 in the city. Often, the Planning Department, for purposes of analysis, will create "pseudo-tracts" in order to differentiate within 1980 Census Tracts which are large in size and/or population.

Parcel Information. The "Site Profile" shows information on any parcel (lot) in the city, by either address (when available) or parcel number. This system is a set of several screens showing data on Land Use, Areas and Districts, Business Licenses, Water Utilities, and Ownership. UIS data elements include:

Address
Assessor's parcel number (APN)
Census Tract
Block
Zoning classification
Acres
Land use code
Council district
Community plan area
Street frontage feet
Number of structures
Total square feet and number of floors (if non-vacant parcel)
Business license information (including status of approvals)
Utility account number and information
List of special districts serving the parcel
Owner's name and mailing address

Land value and improvement value

Other standard assessor's data elements such as tax status and legal description

The "Development Monitoring System" (DMS) is an automated system which tracks the processing of permits. It also extracts information from these permits to forecast changes in urban development (See "System Use" section). The Permits file in DMS includes the following information:

- Tentative subdivision map—recording of information about new maps and their progression through hearings up to final discretionary approval/denial.
- Final subdivision map—recording of information about subdivision maps after they become final
- Rezonings—information about requests, including anticipated number of dwelling units
- Special permits—including Hillside Review, Planned Residential Development, and Conditional Use.

For each of permit types above, DMS documents hearing dates, times, and decisions, plus applicant's name, engineer, location, and owner of land. The Permits file is a hierarchical system with information common to all permit types entered first, then monitoring points for each different type of permit. Permit data is entered by the Planning Department.

Vacant Land Definition. Land use code is based on an original field survey done in the early 1970's. Land use information is updated through the linkage of building permit information with the assessor's records.

UIS does not attempt to define "buildable" or "developable" vacant land because what may be developable to one builder will not be developable to another. The vacant land definition does have, as is evident above, qualifiers attached, such as street frontage, hillside review, zoning, tax rate districts (indication of public services provided to area).

There is often a fine line between agriculturally classified land and vacant land. Currently, there are 20,400 acres classified as agricultural, nonvacant land. Much of this could be converted to vacant classification for purposes of analysis because much agricultural land around San Diego is marginal, one-crop farming.

The amount of vacant land supply available for development has been challenged in the past by developers on grounds of whether vacant land is really usable or buildable (hillside review and street frontage data elements seek to answer this criticism).

Updates. Permit activity is currently updated daily by two Planning Department staff members. Updating of the "Site Profile" is contingent on the assignment of Parcel Identification Numbers (PIN's) to new parcels/lots. The County Assessor's office, because they are oriented to batch processing at the current time, takes anywhere from 2 weeks to 2 months to assign new PIN's and block numbers.

System Use

Outputs. The system provides periodic summary reports plus special computer runs based on specific inquiries. Periodic summary reports include:

Residential and Population Impact Reports. For each community planning area (or other geographic area), estimated residential unit increase or population increase (over and above existing conditions) due to: units under construction, final maps (approved, considered), tentative maps (approved, considered), rezonings (approved, considered), special permits (approved, considered), total impact forecast due to all above. Residential development (existing and in 'pipeline') is then compared to community plan build-out potential by preparing raw figure tabulations and bar graph displays. Forecasted time of 'pipeline' development is determined by type of permit and stage within that permit process.

Population and Land Use Bulletin. Shows, for each community planning area, residential construction activity, housing inventory, general land use acreage, and population and occupied housing units. Published twice a year.

An example of a special computer run based on a specific inquiry is the "City Growth Capacity" report of March 6, 1984. In this report, the development capacity of the city was figured based on community plans and/or zoning classifications. This capacity was then compared to projected residential population growth through the year 1995.

Data Sources. The main sources of data for UIS are the assessor's records (County Assessor's Department), building permit information (Building Inspection Department), and subdivision and tract maps (Planning Department). The assessor's records are the source for the Parcel Identification Number, ownership, and tax information. Land use data is updated through the linking of building permit and subdivision information with the assessor's records. Other sources of information include city utilities and business licensing information.

Users and Uses. *Operating departments:* UIS is used to perform professional and technical tasks in a variety of departments, including Planning, Financial Management, Budget, Engineering and Development, Building Inspection, and Police Departments. Planning uses UIS to monitor the development capacity of the city and to track the development permit process. The UIS coordinator is housed in the Planning Department and is funded through a special account included with Non-Departmental Expenses.

Elected officials: all council members currently have on-line terminals in their staff offices, but most council members route requests to the City Manager or Planning Director, who may refer them to the UIS coordinator or their staffs for analysis and reply. Direct on-line access by policy makers to information would help to cut down costs, but problems of user training and possible misinterpretation of data remain. Elected officials use periodic summary report information more often than requesting special computer runs on a particular topic.

Private sector: use has been mainly by title insurance companies, financing agencies, developers, and realtors. Information has been used as development input to marketing studies, as "lead-finder" by developers searching for buildable land, as source of background information, and for tracking activity of competitor development firms (is a certain area becoming over-saturated with a specific residential building type?). Examples of private sector use of UIS discovered during the case study visit:

- Source of background information, as a starting point for more detailed parcel-specific studies in future. Helpful in discovering what special districts (and associated developer fees) developer would have to deal with if building on that parcel.
- Valuable as a tool in searching for properties, as a "lead-finder"
- Used by a large realty firm for a market study of commercial and residential opportunities around downtown area. Examining subdivisions (tentative and final maps) as opportunities for buying properties which fit the needs of realtor's clients. This firm is planning to initiate their own vacant land parcel computerized database in the future.
- Used by a multi-family development firm to keep track of rezonings, subdivisions in a specified area in order to: purchase properties that have already been rezoned to multi-family or which have been subdivided, look for areas adjacent to parcels which have been rezoned to multi-family. Also used to keep track of competitors in specified areas (is a particular area oversaturated or primed for multi-family development?)

UIS-Growth Management Program Link. The intent of the Growth Management Program, initiated in the late 1970's, was to put enough land in Urbanized and Planned Urbanizing Areas to accommodate the city's share of regional growth until at least 1995. The objective was not to restrict future growth in amount, but to channel it to more easily and economically served locations. The growth management program created three tiers: Urbanized Areas (city pays for needed infrastructure), Planned Urbanizing Areas (service needs met by fees incorporated into development agreements), and Future Urbanizing Areas (no development allowed until 1995).

To assure that there would be an adequate supply of land planned for urban development, City Council directed the Planning Department to report on the growth of the City annually and to evaluate the effect of that growth upon the availability of land. As a benchmark, City Council established the policy that there should be sufficient land planned for urbanization to accommodate the growth projected to occur within the next fifteen years. The Housing Element of the City Progress Guide and General Plan states that there should be a 15-20 year supply of land planned for development at any given time. The draft Housing Element revision currently being considered by City Council provides that an inventory of appropriate sites, suitably distributed throughout the City, should be maintained at a level equal to 2.5 times the City's annual growth needs.

The need for making more land available for development in the Urbanized and Planned Urbanizing Areas is to be reviewed at least annually as a result of the settlement between the City and the Pacific Legal Foundation. Council Policy No. 600-7, set to begin in 1985, states:

It shall further be the policy of the City Council that development in the City shall be monitored, at least on an annual basis, in order to determine the amount of development that has occurred in the Urbanizing and Planned Urbanizing areas; the amount and capacity of the land in these areas remaining for development; the rate of growth and development purposes and how the City is meeting that demand. This data and information shall be used to document the need for City-initiated shifts in land from the Future Urbanizing to the Planned Urbanizing area; to establish whether required findings for approval of development or for owner initiated requests have been met; and to support the necessary General Plan amendments associated with such shifts.

Growth Management Review Task Force. In 1984, the Mayor appointed a "blue ribbon" task force to review the effect of the 1979 Growth Management upon the City after the first five years. As part of the task force, the Subcommittee on Residential Capacity examined existing community plan residential capacities, analyzed public facilities and services, and surveyed community desires. As part of that analysis, five recommendations were made regarding the Development Monitoring System (DMS). They were:

- Devise more sophisticated means of measuring residential capacity and adequacy of community services.
- Redraw residential statistical areas to permit a logical aggregation of relevant land use criteria by statistical area.
- Devise a constraint matrix that measures adequacy of all General Plan-defined land use criteria by statistical area.
- Provide City's DMS with capability of correlating development trends with availability of services.
- Survey public perceptions of levels of community services and quality of life on regular basis and incorporate results with City's DMS.

UIS Budget. Annual operating budget typically ranges from $250,000 to $350,000 for the City's share of total expenses. This includes all database maintenance, transaction and reporting costs, as well as the labor and other costs of design and development of new systems and applications. UIS budget is funded through non-departmental expenses and flows through two accounts, the system coordinator in the Planning Department, and the system administrator in the Data Processing Corporation.

Access and Security. On-line access to system information; responses to queries shown on CRT screens; most computer programs are menu-driven, allowing the user to access different system components, or to access specified subsets of the entire database.

Three levels of security are used: terminal (only certain access points can retrieve certain information), password (only certain users can access and/or update system information), and reporting program security.

Pipeline Tracking. Development Monitoring System (DMS) has automated the tracking of permit processing. Summary information for a specified geographic area and parcel specific information can be obtained for rezonings, subdivisions, and special permits (with each application broken down into proposed and approved).

Private Sector Information System Relationships. No modem access to private sector firms is possible at this time, nor is any planned for the future due to potential security problems. Phone-in requests from private sector are usually handled by the UIS system coordinator in Planning, or other staff members.

The City manager has written a directive stating that only information produced in the "normal course of operations" should be distributed to private interests needing information. This is due to the fact that government is unable to charge a market rate for special computer runs tailored to private sector requests. A California state law states that a public body can only charge on a cost recovery basis for information (this would include compensation for computer time and report generating costs).

The City is sure that information has commercial value, but is unsure of how to distribute to the private sector on an on-line basis. Questions remain as to:

- if on-line access to private sector is on an subscription basis, do private users pay a deposit against which costs are subtracted, or is there a credit card number which user can charge against?
- how does information supplier tell user how much money they are using, or have used?
- who provides the training, technical support, and user service for private users?

System Problems

UIS has experienced the following problems during the design and operation stages:

UIS tended to be a clone of the pre-existing manual system. Thus, inefficiencies that existed in the manual system tended to be copied into the automated system. "You can't just automate the manual system, but have to modify the pre-existing system's procedures and content."

UIS added a layer of work to manual labor, rather than trying to replace the manual work with the automated system. If system adds another layer of data capture on top of existing manual labor, people tasked to do it won't because it won't be something they depend upon to do their day-to-day work.

Functional requirements of user departments were not fully studied and not incorporated into the design of UIS. Thus, departments such as Building Inspection have found certain data entry tasks to be extraneous to the department role/mission. There was no steering committee during the development of UIS to make sure data entry tasks were an integral part of user departments' day-to-day tasks. The lack of a steering committee hurt the interdepartmental coordination of UIS.

Parcel identification is problematic because of non-standardization of street addresses across space, and due to variance of address and legal descriptions over time. This latter problem creates problem of linking history.

Coordination across departments has been problematic. "There is no universal descriptive unit, good for purposes of all user departments." Building Inspection Department often does not enter permits into system because automated system was not made an integral part of the Department's work schedule. Some automated tasks assigned to Building Inspection were not part of that department's main goal or mission.

When the system was first established, planners below management level did not know goals of the system. Some planners had the impression that "keyboard sitting is clerical, not professional." Planners' interaction with computerized system is currently limited. Microcomputers could increase planners' use of the system, but limited time during day makes it hard to do front end work necessary to learning microcomputer hardware and software.

There has been unneeded specialization of the system components. Permit screens originally were broken into four different types (tentative maps, final maps, rezonings, special permits). This created a lot of unneeded specialization because four different databases was not needed. When manual system becomes automated, aggregation of functions (not fragmentation) should occur. UIS currently is changing to a hierarchical permit database, with information common to all permits established first, with monitoring points for each type of permit.

A move to a distributive computer system (subsets of the large database and separate hardware available to different user departments according to their needs) is not likely due to DPC's desire to maintain centralized control of automation. The move to micro- or minicomputers distributed throughout departments has been made less beneficial since DPC has put all data management programs on the mainframe, with interactive capabilities and analytical tools (SAS). DPC would probably not be receptive to the computer decentralization created by a micro- or mini- environment. Another important factor mitigating against a move from centralized to distributed data processing is the sheer size of the databases which are involved. Even with the very large databases involved, however, it appears that some distribution of processing and specialization is likely to occur as San Diego incorporates interactive computerized mapping into the system. The software and hardware environment in which geographic information systems have most successfully evolved is primarily a minicomputer one. In part this is because the intensive mathematical computational power needed for geographic processing has been available on minicomputer systems.

System Improvements

The developing Regional Urban Information System (RUIS) is providing the City of San Diego with the opportunity to improve and enhance the existing UIS. Some RUIS improvements include:

Future hardware improvements with RUIS will revolve around a computer mapping system. San Diego Gas & Electric has implemented a county-wide automated facilities mapping program on an IBM mainframe, and the RUIS task force has expressed an interest in this package. The SDG & E system is a computer drafting system linked to a database for the facilities and parcel information. A geographic information element in RUIS would mean that the automated parcel system would be tied to invariant geographic identifiers, in addition to variant identifiers such as addresses or assessor's parcel numbers. Such a system would use polygons, points, and/or lines to geographically identify parcel boundaries.

A steering committee is paralleling the development and design of RUIS, not coming in post-hoc. The prominent characteristics of this task force are:

- All proposed and potential users of the system are involved in the design phase.
- There is management level commitment to the steering committee. In this way, budgetary and personnel changes required by RUIS can be realized.
- There is a single system coordinator for each jurisdiction (city and county) responsible for the system development and operation.
- Below the management level steering committee, there are middle level subcommittees composed of technical staff within the proposed user departments. These subcommittees are working on the technical details of the system, such as land use coding, property identification, and name standards. Proposed day-to-day users of the RUIS are well represented on these subcommittees.
- There is a central organization (DPC) and a single coordinator for each jurisdiction whose job it is to coordinate the varying needs of the committee members/departments.

The functional requirements of potential user departments are being analyzed during the RUIS design phase. The city and county has hired Environmental Systems Research Institute to do a conceptual design for RUIS. ESRI's 4-step development process is as follows:

- Extensive interviewing and data gathering from potential user departments in order to gain a focused understanding of how current operational activities are performed.
- Determination of automated system functional requirements - hardware and software types required to support operational activities outlined in the first step.
- Creation and analysis of alternative database and system designs.
- Recommended design solution and preparation of a conceptual implementation strategy and budget estimate, and the provision of a final design solution to the steering committee.

The creation of an independent, chartered, non-profit agency to house RUIS is a possibility for the future. This might allow the charging of market rates for the information and would probably increase the marketing of such information and its distribution. Because higher rates would be charged the private sector, the government could get services from the non-profit agency at less than cost, which would help the governments of the city and county in meeting Proposition 4 expenditure limitations.

Further Information

Publications
Environmental Systems Research Institute, "Regional Urban Information System Conceptual Design," May 1985.
  Volume 1: Summary Findings
  Volume 2: Organization Summaries and Interview Report
Data Processing Corporation, Committee on Physical Development, "Data Processing Systems Master Plan," undated.

Contact

Tim O'Connell
System Coordinator–UIS/RUIS
San Diego City Planning Department
City Administration Building
San Diego, CA 92101
Telephone: (619) 236-6367

Appendix B

Characteristics of 24 Public
Land Supply Information Systems

Agency: **ASSOCIATION OF BAY AREA GOVERNMENTS (ABAG)**

System Name: Local Development Policy Survey

Type of System: Manual

Objectives: To identify and quantify available land for development; land supply estimates will be used in making subregional forecasts of population, households, and employment

Data Sources: Interviews with local planning departments; local records and maps

Coverage: 9-county San Francisco Bay area

Information Collected for Vacant Land:

Location
Land acreage
Existing land use
Type of development/redevelopment occurring 1975-1980
Type development opportunity/unavailable open land
Forecasted time of development
Sewer, water, roads existing, committed, planned
Census tract
Local Agency Formation Commission (LAFCO) sphere of influence
Zoning and General Plan designation

Qualifiers Attached to Vacant Land Definition: "Available"/"unavailable", based on relevant jurisdictions' zoning and general plan policies

Updating: Two surveys done, in 1976 and 1981-1982

Main Government Users: ABAG itself for small area population projections: cities use data, which is aggregated by census tracts or communities, in general plan reviews and forecasts

Private Sector Use: Limited

Estimate of Costs: $80,000 for 1981/82 survey; costs were higher for 1976 survey

Contact: Susan Hootkins
ABAG
P.O. Box 2050
Oakland, CA 94604
(415) 464-7928

Jurisdiction Name: **CHARLOTTE, NORTH CAROLINA**

System Name: Data Management System/Small Area Geographic System (system is currently being developed)

Type of System: Mainframe, with ADR Datacomp DP database manager

Objectives: To provide Planning Department with land use data during mid-Census years; used to estimate growth trends

Data Sources: Census, land use, building permit, and employment files merged into a common database

Coverage: Mecklenburg County

Information Collected for Vacant Land:
Parcel number
Presence of public services (water, sewer, utilities, electric, gas)
Topography
Zoning and General Plan designation
Origin and Destination Zone
Census Tract
Existing land use
Land and improvement value
Situs Address
Building permit data (type of residential permit)

Qualifiers Attached to Vacant Land Definition: subdivided, not subdivided, water areas, under construction

Updating: Annually (forecasted)

Main Government Users: Planning Department (statistical analyses, summarization of trends, rank-ordering)

Private Sector Use: Strong demand for information expected from private sector (especially marketing analysts)

Estimate of Costs: $5,000/year for operational costs

Contact: Steve Patterson
        Municipal Information Systems Department
        301 S. McDowall St., Suite 300
        Charlotte, NC 28204
        (704) 336-2914

Jurisdiction Name: **CONTRA COSTA COUNTY, CALIFORNIA**

System Name: Land Information System

Type of System: Mainframe/Micro with IDMS mainframe database manager and vendor-produced micro software

Objectives: To provide a common database for all county government departments; to increase efficiency between and within departments; to provide better service to public during building permit and planning application process

Data Sources: Assessor's parcel file, zoning maps and ordinances, General Plan designation, Planning Department environmental maps, building inspection data, contractors information on file in Building Inspection, and public works data

Coverage: all of unincorpoated County, some of incorporated areas (approximately 280,000 parcels)

Information Collected for Vacant Land

   Parcel number
   Parcel history (public actions on that parcel)
   To-From (showing 'parent' or 'child' parcel numbers)
   Tax rate area (code designating each unique combination of taxing districts)
   Primary and secondary owners
   Land and improvement values

Situs description
Situs address
Notification address
Census tract
Supervisorial district
Seismic zone
Flood hazard zone
Land use code
Acreage
Drainage fee
Zoning
General Plan area and designation
Permits for building inspection, planning applications, and public works
   permits

Qualifiers Attached to Vacant Land Definition: "Unbuildable" designation
based on particular land use policies of the relevant jurisdiction

Updating: Day-to-day

Main Government Users: County departments such as Assessment, Building
Inspection, Planning, Public Works; also, 6 cities have on-line access to LIS
and can do their own inputting/updating

Private Sector Use: County plans to encourage private sector on-line access in
the future. User charge per terminal has been established

Estimate of Costs: Development costs estimated to be: $58,000 (1981-82),
$295,000 (1982-83), $348,000 (1983-84), $795,000 (1984-85). Operational costs
per year estimated in feasibility report to be: $368,600 (first year)-$448,036
(fifth year)

Contact: Bob Nash, LIS Director
          651 Pine St., 8th Floor
          Martinez, CA 94553
          (415) 372-2386

Jurisdiction Name: **DALLAS**

System Name: Vacant Parcel File

Type of System: Mainframe

Objectives: To assist private developers in identifying infill opportunities,
especially for residential purposes

Data Sources: Assessor's tax records

Coverage: City of Dallas (approximately 40,000 parcel records)

Information Collected for Vacant Land:

Parcel address
Census tract
Legal description
Community designation (for CDBG-eligible areas)
Taxpayer's name
Zoning
Front footage
Infrastructure (alleys and utilities-water, sewer, gas, and electricity)
Streets (improved or unimproved)

Qualifiers Attached to Vacant Land Definition: None; vacant = no improvement value

Updating: Hard copy extracts of assessor records produced in 1979 and 1980

Main Government Users: Oriented to private sector use

Private Sector Use: Developers and realtors; computer printouts 20 cents per page to private sector

Contact: Jim Calhoun
Dept. of Housing and Urban Rehabilitation
City Hall
1500 Marilla
Dallas, TX 75201
(214) 670-3602

Jurisdiction Name: **DENVER**

System Name: Land Use Information System

Type of System: Mainframe/Micro; use of R-base 4000 on micro

Objectives: Originally, to obtain a snapshot of land use and zoning characteristics as part of Federal community renewal program; to detail how land use/housing characteristics have changed over time

Data Sources: Assessor's records, zoning and subdivision records, title information

Coverage: City/County of Denver (approximately 165,000 parcels)

Information Collected for Vacant Land:

Assessor's number
Situs address
Land use code
Zoning
Parcel size
Assessed value (land and improvements)
Last three sales dates
Last three sales amounts
Census tract/block
Neighborhood Council District

Qualifiers Attached to Vacant Land Definition: "Developable" definition based on qualitative studies, not incorporated into system

Updating: Annually; new extract from assessor's file created annually through batch processing

Main Government Users: Information has supported Planning Department; primarily an internal tool for government; also used by utility companies

Private Sector Use: Limited; private non-profit organizations; standard reports are available for public inspection

Estimate of Costs: Development costs for planning office only estimated to be $100,000 plus $50,000 for computer time; operational costs for updating estimated to be $5,000 for data processing and $5,400 for labor costs

Contact: Dennis Siglinger
    Denver Planning Office—Data Services Division
    1445 Cleveland Place
    Denver, CO 80202
    (303) 575-2838

Jurisdiction Name: **FAIRFAX COUNTY, VIRGINIA**

System Name: Urban Development Information System

Type of System: Mainframe, with in-house computer programs, SAS, and EASYTRIEVE software

Objectives: To monitor growth and make short term forecasts of housing and population by small areas, to translate annual forecasts into demand for public facilities, to analyze demand forecasts to project timing and location needs for new public facilities

Data Sources: Real estate land master file, rezoning application system, plan and agreement monitoring system, building permit application system, sewer network coding printout

Coverage: All parcels in County

Information Collected for Vacant Land:

Map reference number
Planning district
Street address
Subdivision name
Land area of parcel
Zoning information
Building permit info
Stage of development
Underutilized and vacant acreage of parcel
Site plan or subdivision plan information
Parcel sewer identification information
Supervisor district
Sewershed
Subcensus tract
Dwelling unit count
Existing land use of parcel
Assessment information
Planned land use of parcel
Gross floor area

Qualifiers Attached to Vacant Land Definition: "vacant" (no improvement or dilapidated structure) and "underutilized" (current density is less than potential density)

Updating: Tax records annually, permits and housing starts daily

Main Government Users: Office of Waste Management, Department of Public Works; Fairfax County Water Authority; Office of Comprehensive Planning; Department of Environmental Management; Office of Assessments

Private Sector Use: High use; 20 documents (15,000 copies) of UDIS-generated information are used by public each year; presence of private land supply information providers

Estimate of Costs: Development costs for pilot test project in 1970 carried by HUD ($125,000) and County ($140,000); additional federal funding of $246,000 and County funding of $244,000 was used to extend system to the entire County

Contact: George Kohut, Data Processing Manager
Office of Research and Statistics
4100 Chain Bridge Road
Fairfax, VA 22030
(703) 691-2355

Jurisdiction Name: **HOUSTON**

System Name: Metropolitan Common Data Base (Metrocom)

Type of System: Interactive graphing system ("Synercom") and minicomputer

Objectives: To assist the Department of Public Works, and to speed up the revenue collection procedure

Data Sources: Tax assessor's records, building permit data, plat information, public works sewer line maps, aerial photos (for digitization of curves and irregular features)

Coverage: All parcels within Houston city limits (recent annexations have not been included in database yet)

Information Collected for Vacant Land:

Tax assessor's records
Land use code
Assessed value (land and improvements)
Sewer network
Water lines
Presence of roads

Qualifiers Attached to Vacant Land Definition: None (vacant = no structure)

Updating: Once/year (recent annexed land not always incorporated into Metrocom database)

Main Government Users: Public Works and Tax Departments

Private Sector Use: Government plans to market information to private sector in future, but database needs to be cleaned up

Estimate of Costs: Estimated $22-25 million over 10 year period

Contact: Joe Chow
Houston Planning Department
P.O. Box 1562
Houston, TX 77251
(713) 222-3261

Jurisdiction Name: **JACKSONVILLE, FLORIDA**

System Name: Unnamed (system is in development stage)

Type of System: Micro-based, with Lotus 1-2-3, "Smart" database manager, and Statpro software scheduled to be used

Objectives: To estimate transportation needs demand and impact of growth on existing infrastructure; to provide database which can be used by developers

Data Sources: Tax assessor's records, building permit data, electricity hook-ups

Coverage: Parts of Jacksonville/Duval County (initial focus is on high growth southeastern district)

Information Collected for Vacant Land:

Census tract
Planning district
Traffic analysis zones
Assessment information
Land use code (if vacant, whether land is "developable" or not)
Additional information (data elements still in planning stage)

Qualifiers Attached to Vacant Land Definition: "Developable" land = vacant (−) wetlands (−) developed land

Updating: Frequency unknown at this time

Main Government Users: Slated to be used internally by staff and by elected officials

Private Sector Use: Possible users include developers, marketing analysts, Chamber of Commerce

Estimate of Costs: Development costs (so far) are estimated to be $3500 for hardware and $4000 for software

Contact: Harry Learner or Barbara Barsh
Jacksonville Planning Department
128 E. Forsyth St., Suite 700
Jacksonville, FL 32202
(904) 633-2690

Jurisdiction Name: **KING COUNTY, WASHINGTON**

System Name: Land Development Information System

Type of System: Mainframe (originally manual tabulations)

Objectives: To provide mechanism to monitor effect of county policy and land use regulations on the land market; base of demographic and land use information

Data Sources: Tax records, building permit information, subdivision information, forecasts from Puget Sound COG; large-scale reference maps being phased out as a source

Coverage: Developable portion of King County west of the Cascade Mountains. Approximately 800 square miles

Information Collected for Vacant Land:

Acreage
Zoning (6 categories)
Landslide, seismic, and wetlands constraints
Land use code (includes vacant-constrained definition)
Sewer service availability
Jurisdiction
Census tract
Quarter-section (also township and range)
Community planning area

Qualifiers Attached to Vacant Land Definition: 2 levels of vacant land based on county regulations—unconstrained and constrained (by physical hazards)

Updating: Building permits—weekly; reclassifications—quarterly; vacant land inventory—1980 and 1983

Main Government Users: Predominantly the planning division, but also useful to a wide range of public agencies

Private Sector Use: Annual growth reports put out by the King County planning division are used by developers, appraisers, realtors, community groups

Estimate of Cost: Preparation of annual growth reports is a "two-person-a-year" job, with an annual budget of about $75,000

Contact: Chandler Felt
LDIS Acting Director
King County Planning Division
700 Alaska Building, 618 Second Ave.
Seattle, WA 98104
(206) 344-7550

Jurisdiction Name: **LANE COUNTY, OREGON**

System Name: Regional Information System

Type of System: Mainframe (IBM 3033), with computerized mapping module

Objectives: To provide geographic information system primarily, but not solely, for Planning and Public Works Departments of county and city governments. To monitor the amount of vacant land available within Urban Growth Boundaries

Data Sources: Assessor's tax file and digitized assessor's maps; updated through building permit and subdivision information; also field checks and aerial photos

Coverage: County-wide (approximately 4,610 square miles)

Information Collected for Vacant Land:

Acreage
Zoning and General Plan designation
Sales data (used for analyzing sales trends and land availability)
Digitized perimeters and parcel centroid
Soils, floodplain, and slope limitations
Forecasted time of development, based on whether a parcel is inside or out-
    side a city
Census tracts and blocks
Jurisdiction
Special district
Other geographic entities

Qualifiers Attached to Vacant Land Definition: "Undeveloped" (no improvement value) broken into two categories:

"Developable"–zoned properly, larger than ½ acre.
"Buildable"–subdivided or partitioned, zoned properly, between minimum
    lot size and ½ acre

Updating: Annually by batch processing

Main Government Users: Planning, Public Works, Assessment, Taxation, Police; approximately 350 terminals connected to database

Private Sector Use: Main access to system at the Development Assistance Counter in the Eugene Development Department. Use by developers, appraisers, and planning consultants

Estimate of Costs: Five person years of work for development (included $50,000 from HUD and $30,000 from Lane COG and city of Eugene). Maintenance costs originally were $55,000/year. By 1984-1985, this estimate up to $114,000 (not including assessor's work)

Contact: Jim Carlson, Program Manager–Research
       Lane Council of Governments
       125 E. 8th Avenue
       Eugene, OR 97401
       (503) 687-4283

Jurisdiction Name: **LOS ANGELES**

System Name: Land Use Planning And Management System (LUPAMS)

Type of System: Mainframe

Objectives: Provision of parcel data for multiple uses and multiple departments

Data Sources: County Assessor's data, building permit and subdivision information, parcel land area and planned land use extracted from City Clerk and Planning Department files

Coverage: City of Los Angeles

Information Collected for Vacant Land:

Parcel Identification Number
Parcel address
Zoning
Tax code area
Market land and improvement value
Last sale amount
Owner's name and mailing address
Parcel area
Census tract

Council district
Community number
Land use code (existing)
Planned land use
Zoning corrections
Inside/outside city limit
Public or private ownership

Qualifiers Attached to Vacant Land Definition: No physical hazard qualifiers attached to vacant definition

Updating: Every 6 months

Main Government Users: Data Services Bureau of City Clerk's Office and Planning Department are main users

Private Sector Use: Current use by private sector of a file from the County Assessor's records. File contains land use code and last 2 sales prices

Contact: Dan Gallagher
Chief–LUPAMS
Los Angeles City Clerk's Office
Los Angeles, CA 90012
(213) 485-5741

Agency Name: **MIAMI VALLEY (OHIO) REGIONAL PLANNING COMMISSION**

System Name: Land Capability Analysis

Type of System: State database (Ohio Capability Analysis) assessed by RPC. Maps for each county, and statistical analyses done on mainframe

Objectives: To provide environmental information for the 208 Water Quality Management program in the mid-1970's

Data Sources: State Department of Natural Resources files (OCAP), aerial photos, field surveys, other records and maps for specialized data such as flooding and soils

Coverage: 5-county Miami Valley surrounding Dayton

Information Collected for Vacant Land:

Existing land use
Soil information

Landcover
Slope
Groundwater availability
Bedrock depth
Political boundaries
Watersheds
Traffic zones
Census tracts

Qualifiers Attached to Vacant Land Definition: Suitability of vacant land for development determined by a linear regression model using over 30 independent variables

Updating: One-time only in 1975, no updating since due to staff and budget cutbacks

Main Government Users: Use by elected officials to revise Miami Valley Land Use Plan

Private Sector Use: Summary reports were available to public. Private sector use of information limited because system is not parcel-specific

Estimate of Costs: "Very costly"; development costs shared by state and Regional Planning Agency

Contact: Larry Perrin
Mapping/Graphics
Miami Valley RPC
117 South Main
Dayton, OH 45402
(513) 223-6323

Jurisdiction Name: **MINNEAPOLIS (METRO COUNCIL)**

System Name: Unnamed

Type of System: Originally manual; currently being automated to a mainframe system

Objectives: To measure the amount of vacant land and rate of consumption relative to available supply. To provide information for systems planning (sewers, transit, highways, parklands)

Data Sources: Aerial photos, augmented by building permit and subdivision information, also business directories. Computerization will introduce census information, soil data, and tax assessor's information as sources

Coverage: 7-county metropolitan area

Information Collected for Vacant Land:

Watershed
Floodplain
Slope estimates
Jurisdiction
Sector (8 tabulation units)
Geocodes include county, city, ring, and sector (the four rings are central city, fully developed suburbs, developing suburbs, and the outer area)
Inside/outside Urban Services Area
Digitized perimeters (in future)

Qualifiers Attached to Vacant Land Definition: vacant, with some restraints (physical hazards such as floodplains); no attempt at defining "buildable" because definition varies with user

Updating: Vacant land inventories done in 1980 and 1984

Main Government Users: Comprehensive Planning Department, Environmental section (sewers, solid waste), Transportation Department, Metropolitan Airports Commission, Metro Council

Private Sector Use: Developers, marketing analysts, planning consultants. Parcel-specific information would have to be retrieved from appropriate local government, not part of Metro land use inventory

Estimate of Costs: Aerial photos cost $35,000 for 1984 update of inventory; update required one person-year of work; current digitization estimated to cost $15,000 every 3 years

Contact: Michael Munson
Program Manager for Research
Metropolitan Council of the Twin Cities
300 Metro Square Bldg.
7th and Robert
St. Paul, MN 55101
(612) 291-6331

Jurisdiction Name: **MONTGOMERY COUNTY, MARYLAND**

System Name: Vacant Land Data Bank

Type of System: Minicomputer (Hewlett Packard 3000), with micros (Hewlett Packard 9000 and 150) used for graphics and as terminals

Objectives: To estimate the amount of land supply in each of the zoning categories; to forecast future development potential; to analyze cost of housing in various areas of county

Data Sources: Tax assessor's parcel file, supplemented with information from the planning department. Other inputs include a definition of vacant land, estimated dwelling unit yields per acre for each residential zone, and current developer land use plans for planned community zones

Coverage: County-wide (approximately 380,000 parcels)

Information Collected for Vacant Land:

    Acreage
    Land assessment
    Improvement assessment
    Land use code
    Vacant land definition
    Zoning
    Dwelling unit potential
    Census tract and block
    Planning area
    Sewer category
    Traffic zone
    Drainage basin
    Policy area

Qualifiers Attached to Vacant Land Definition: vacant land defined as: parcels with no improvement value, farm assessed land, or partially vacant (or redevelopable) parcels with land value greater than improvement value

Updating: Parcel and subdivision files quarterly, building permits monthly

Main Government Users: Research Division, Community Plans Division, Housing and Community Development Department, Housing Opportunities Commission, Office of Economic Development

Private Sector Use: Major users are realtors (garden apartments and commercial), strong use of system by private sector; 50 cents per page costs to private sector to recover costs

Contact: Drew Dedrick, Research Division
        Montgomery County Planning Board
        8787 Georgia Avenue
        Silver Spring, MD 20907
        (301) 495-4700

Jurisdiction Name: **NEW HAVEN**

System Name: Land Use Information System (LUIS)

Type of System: Micro based system (Altos 586, TRS-80, and IBM PC-AT); software includes UNIFY and SOLIR

Objectives: To track progress of both individual cases (parcel-specific) and entire program activity; to understand housing market demand; to provide indicators of community well-being and needs

Data Sources: Property address list, assessment information, DIME File/Geocoding, city permits, property transfers, code violation, liens, housing program activity, business activity, census information

Coverage: All of New Haven's 26,000 land parcels

Information Collected for Vacant Land:

Address
Ownership
Back taxes
Code violations
Sales data
Background Census data
Neighborhood and ward
Assessed valuation
Existing land use
Fires
Building permits
Mortgage information
Census tract
X-Y coordinates

Qualifiers Attached to Vacant Land Definition: Vacant land parcels can be identified which have back taxes or liens

Updating: Assessor's list yearly, building permits monthly, and property transfers biweekly

Main Government Users: Office of Housing and Neighborhood Development; other agencies include Downtown/Harbor, Real Estate Services, and Economic Development. Used to locate infill opportunities and to analyze housing and neighborhood activity

Private Sector Use: Very little use by private sector thus far. Lists of abandoned buildings beneficial to realtors

Estimate of Costs: Development costs approximately $118,000 (including $43,000 for programmer/analysts and $40,000 for hardware and software). Operating budget estimated to be $72,000 (including $42,000 for staff salaries and $25,000 for programmer/analysts)

Contact: Daniel Kops
        Coordinator, Information System Development
        Office of Housing and Neighborhood Development
        157 Church St.
        New Haven, CT 06510
        (203) 787-7090

Jurisdiction Name: **PHOENIX**

System Name: Village Traffic Analysis Zone Profiles

Type of System: Manual system currently; plan to use microcomputer in future

Objectives: To monitor development in each of the nine Urban Villages

Data Sources: Census summary tape file information, land use maps and inventories, zoning and subdivision maps, field surveys, Maricopa Association of Governments forecasts. Building permit data will be used to update if microcomputer used in future

Coverage: Phoenix city plus COG-designated "Municipal Planning Area" beyond the current city limits

Information Collected for Vacant Land:

  Zoning (4 residential categories)
  Watershed and wash areas
  Forecasted time of development
  Traffic analysis zone
  Urban village
  Census tract and block
  Land withheld (publicly owned)

Qualifiers Attached to Vacant Land Definition: "Developable" = vacant or agricultural land not reserved or withheld; "Land reserved" = in floodplains, wash areas, or airport expansion areas, or land which is publicly owned

Updating: Inventory done in 1980 and 1982

Main Government Users: Planning staff (Research Division), council members primary users of information

Private Sector Use: Used by COG planning consultant in locating employment centers for purposes of computer demand modelling

Estimate of Costs: Planning Department is proposing the purchase of an IBM PC-AT with hard disk, and Encore! software. Development cost for this proposed enhancement is $30,000. Estimated maintenance costs are $3,500/year. Current manual update takes about 4 persons full-time one year. Proposed automated updating estimated to take one person full-time six months

Contact: Bob Johnson
         Planning Department, Research Section
         125 East Washington
         Phoenix, AZ 87004
         (602) 262-4079

Jurisdiction Name: **PORTLAND, OREGON (METRO)**

System Name: Land Inventory

Type of System: UNIX-based microcomputer system

Objectives: To accurately measure land use changes and vacant land supplies and characteristics. To evaluate the role of the Urban Growth Boundary in changing land prices as differentiated from other public policies

Data Sources: Primarily aerial photos, supplemented by building permit records and field surveys

Coverage: 4-county area surrounding Portland

Information Collected for Vacant Land:

  Acreage
  Existing land use
  Zoning (4 residential categories)
  Sewer and water availability
  Hazard areas (predominantly slopes and floodplain)
  Planned land use
  Jurisdiction
  Inside/outside Urban Growth Boundary
  Census tract (land use data is compiled at this level)

Qualifiers Attached to Vacant Land Definition: 2 physical hazard categories applied to vacant land categories

Updating: Since original 1977 inventory, updates have occurred in 1980 and 1983.

Main Government Users: Primarily used for land use and transportation planning.

Private Sector Use: Development community has not used extensively because system is not parcel-specific

Estimate of Costs: 1977 original inventory cost estimated to be $45,000; 1980 update and modification estimated to be $40,000. Operating/maintenance costs estimated to be $75,000/year (including land use, transportation, and forecasting components)

Contact: Dick Bowen
Portland Metro
527 Southwest Hall
Portland, OR 97201
(503) 221-1646

Jurisdiction Name: **SACRAMENTO**

System Name: Vacant Land Survey Update (system is currently being developed)

Type of System: IBM-PC hard disk microcomputer, with D-Base II software

Objectives: To update manual vacant land inventory done in early 1980's. To keep track of growth in certain areas, especially areas which are constrained by a lack of public services. To assist in the development of a Housing Element, as required by California law

Data Sources: County assessor's roll, field surveys and aerials (in certain cases), building department files and permits

Coverage: City of Sacramento

Information Collected for Vacant Land:

(scheduled for inclusion)
Assessor's parcel number
Situs address
Water, sewer, drainage present or not
Floodplains
Zoning

General Plan designation
Traffic zone
Community plan area
Noise impact

Qualifiers Attached to Vacant Land Definition: "Vacant-constrained" = constraining factors include physical hazards and lack of public services

Updating: Frequency not known at this time

Main Government Users: Planning staff and City Council slated to be main government users

Private Sector Use: Planning Department feels that information will be most useful to market analysts

Estimate of Costs: All development work done in-house; expenses thus far paid through the normal budget

Contact: Gary Ziegenfuss
        City Planning Department
        927 10th St.
        Sacramento, CA 95814
        (916) 449-5381

Jurisdiction Name: **SAN DIEGO**

System Name: Urban Information System (UIS)

Type of System: Mainframe (IBM 3031), with interactive mainframe software providing on-line, menu-driven access to user departments

Objectives: To monitor development pressures in order to prepare for public facilities and infrastructure. To monitor the rate of vacant land consumption in the "Urbanized" and "Planned Urbanizing" areas, as set forth in the Growth Management Program

Data Sources: County assessor's records, building permit information, subdivision and tract maps, city utilities and business licensing information

Coverage: Currently, the City of San Diego (approximately ⅓ million parcels). In future, the City of San Diego plus unincorporated areas of San Diego County (approximately 1 million parcels will be in the system at that time)

Information Collected for Vacant Land:

Address
Census tract
Zoning classification
Land use code
Community plan area
Business license information
Utility account number and information
List of special districts serving the parcel
Owner's name and mailing address
Land value and improvement value
Tax status and legal description
Parcel number
Census block
Acreage
Council district
Street frontage feet

Qualifiers Attached to Vacant Land Definition: No attempt to define "buildable" or "developable"; physical hazard and public service constraints on parcel included in system

Updating: Permit activity is updated daily by two Planning Department staff members. New parcel identification numbers and ownership changes from County assessor's office usually take 2 weeks to 2 months

Main Government Users: Planning, Financial Management, Budget, Engineering and Development, Building Inspection, and Police Departments use UIS information. All city council members have on-line access to the system

Private Sector Use: Title insurance companies, financing agencies, developers, and realtors

Estimate of Costs: Annual operating budget typically ranges from $250,000 to $350,000 for the City's share of total expenses. UIS budget is funded through "non-departmental expenses" account

Contact: Tim O'Connell, System Coordinator-UIS
San Diego City Planning Department
City Administration Building
San Diego, CA 92101
(619) 236-6367

Jurisdiction Name: **SAN JOSE**

System Name: Vacant Land Inventory

Type of System: VAX minicomputer, with Inter-Graph software and hardware. Other software used includes "Datatrieve," "SPSS," and "Speakeasy"

Objectives: To provide accurate information on vacant land to devote to accommodating growth – acreage, land use designation, and past activity (trends over time). To help assure that there is an ongoing and adequate supply of land to meet the long-term objectives of the General Plan

Data Sources: Primarily, aerial photos at 1 to 12,000. Digitizing based on base maps of city from the engineering department

Coverage: "Urban Service Area" of San Jose city, as set forth in the General Plan

Information Collected for Vacant Land:

Zoning
General Plan designation
Land use code
Floodway and floodplain
Councilmanic district
Census tract
Special districts serving the area
Other geographic aggregations possible (Inter-Graph allows for flexibility here)

Qualifiers Attached to Vacant Land Definition: Vacant land – inside Urban Service Area

Updating: Annually

Main Government Users: Primarily, internal staff in Information Systems and Planning Departments; vacant land information published and distributed to elected officials

Private Sector Use: Summary reports have been purchased by private parties in the past. Digitized polygon is not tied to assessor's parcel number

Estimate of Costs: Since computerized mapping component added in 1979, an estimated 1½ million dollars has been spent on hardware. Digitizing usually is done by student interns

Contact: Noel Ameele
      San Jose Planning Department
      801 North 1st St.
      San Jose, CA 95110
      (408) 277-5175

Jurisdiction Name: **SANTA CLARA COUNTY, CALIFORNIA**

System Name: Data Base Extension of 2-D

Objectives: To manage the financial accounting of parcels and values over time and combine with mapping and reporting mechanisms

Data Sources: County assessor's records, DIME data, utility records and assessments

Coverage: Central Campbell Redevelopment Area (approximately 500 parcels in a ½ mile by ¾ mile area)

Information Collected for Vacant Land:

   Parcel identification number
   Electricity, utility, and phone account information
   Tax status
   Land value
   Improvement value
   Digitized perimeters (streets, blocks)

Qualifiers Attached to Vacant Land Definition: Tax status (secured or unsecured property)

Updating: Forecasted to be once a year, or as need arises

Main Government Users: Financial Management Department, Planning Department, Center for Urban Analysis

Private Sector Use: Limited thus far

Estimate of Costs: $5,000-10,000 (so far) in staff time to develop a relational model combining parcel-specific data with the DIME Query and Maintenance system

Contact: Frank Lockfeld
         Center for Urban Analysis
         County Government Center
         70 West Hedding St.
         San Jose, CA 95110
         (408) 299-3285

Jurisdiction Name: **STOCKTON, CALIFORNIA**

System Name: Land Use File

Type of System: Mainframe

Objectives: To gather data and keep records on the characteristics of parcels so that statistical analysis can be done on areas of the city. To track the amount of vacant land in the Measure A growth limits

Data Sources: Assessor's records, building permits, subdivision maps, business licenses, use permits, field checks

Coverage: Metropolitan Stockton (most of San Joaquin County is included in the system)

Information Collected for Vacant Land:

Address
Parcel identification number
Census tract and block
Traffic zone
Land use code
Zoning
Inside/outside city limits
Road frontage
Acreage
Structure code (if non-vacant)
Ownership code (private, public, semi-public, etc.)
Month, year checked
Planned Unit Residential Development

Qualifiers Attached to Vacant Land Definition: Vacant land defined as lacking structure and having no improvement value

Updating: Historically, once a year

Main Government Users: Community Development Department (Planning Division), Building Department, Public Works Department; additional departments (such as Fire and Police) currently setting up terminals so they can access Land Use File

Private Sector Use: Development community in past has been critical of the system because it does not analyze the "availability" of vacant land

Contact: Lee Hemminger
Stockton Community Development Dept.
Planning Division
City Hall
Stockton, CA 95202
(209) 944-8266

Jurisdiction Name: **TULSA**

System Name: Land Activity File (discontinued in 1978)

Type of System: Mainframe

Objectives: To monitor development activity in Tulsa County.

Data Sources: Tax assessor's records, building permits, field surveys, aerial photos

Coverage: Tulsa County

Information Collected for Vacant Land:

Parcel number
Situs address
Physical hazards (floodplain, slope, soils)
Census tract
Planning area
Jurisdiction
Traffic zone

Qualifiers Attached to Vacant Land Definition: "Vacant-constrained" based on physical hazards (predominantly floodplains)

Updating: One-time survey in 1977-1978; discontinued due to cost of maintaining; system wasn't designed with maintenance, updating in mind

Main Government Users: Tulsa Planning Department, Tulsa Council of Governments

Private Sector Use: Fairly active use by residential and industrial developers when system was active

Estimate of Costs: System discontinued because of cost considerations, especially updating costs

Contact: Bob Pendergrass
Tulsa Council of Governments
707 S. Houston
Tulsa, OK 74127
(918) 584-7526

Jurisdiction Name: **WASHINGTON, D.C.**

System Name: Municipal Automated Geographic Information System (MAGIS)

Type of System: Mainframe, with software written in-house

Objectives: To track housing activity for CDBG program. To provide an information base for planning purposes

Data Sources: D.C. Real Property Data Bank (assessor's file), recorder deeds file, vacancy inventory (done by Sanborn Map Co.), housing unit study, historic preservation records, permits for new construction, repair, and demolition

Coverage: District of Columbia

Information Collected for Vacant Land:

Lot
Premise address
Land use code
Year of sales and sales price
Assessed land and improvement value
Mortgage, down payment, interest rate
Owner's name and mailing address
Primary zoning code
Census tract and block
Assessment neighborhood
Community development area
Advisory neighborhood commission district
Neighborhood strategy area
Ward

Qualifiers Attached to Vacant Land Definition: "Truly vacant" = lot or parcel not improved with a real property structure; "Falsely vacant" = if an improvement is split by a lot boundary, the assessor assigns the improvement with all its information to one lot, and designates the remaining lot as vacant. The vacant lot is the false vacancy

Updating: Annual (batch updates)

Main Government Users: Predominantly, the Department of Housing and Community Development. Occasional use by elected officials when targeting public programs to specific areas of the District

Private Sector Use: Use by real estate brokers to identify location, sales records, and owner's name and mailing address

Estimate of Costs: Development costs estimated to be $330,000 (CDBG funding). Maintenance costs estimated to be $100,000/year

Contact: Nathan P. Levy, Assistant Chief
Data Services Division
D.C. Office of Planning and Development
Room 451–420 7th Street, N.W.
Washington, DC 20004
(202) 727-6533

Annotated Bibliography

Why Monitor? The Effects of Supply Restrictions and Growth Management on Housing Costs

Black, Tom and Jim Hoben, "Land Price Inflation and Affordable Housing: Causes and Impacts," *Urban Geography*, 1985.

This empirical study of 30 metropolitan areas found that over 80% of the variation in lot price increases between 1975 and 1980 is explainable by a model combining land supply and demand factors. The significant predictor variables (in order of importance) were: 1) index of regulatory restriction, 2) population increases, 3) per capita income increases, 4) job increases.

Dowall, David E., "Reducing the Cost Effects of Local Land Use Controls," *APA Journal*, April 1981.

This paper discusses the two main options when supply in one housing submarket is constrained: redirection of market forces to other submarkets (if seen as viable substitutes), or occurrence of considerable land price inflation (if viable alternative submarkets not present).

Dowall, David E., *The Suburban Squeeze: Land Conversion and Regulation in the San Francisco Bay Area*, University of California Press, Berkeley CA, 1984.

This book examines the tension between housing demand and land use control currently being felt in the San Francisco Bay Area, and views this "suburban squeeze" as a possible harbinger of things to come in such areas as Denver, Tucson, Seattle, Portland, and Washington D.C. The author profiles the historical growth patterns and examines the local land use controls in six Bay Area cities—Fremont, Concord, Napa, Santa Rosa, San Rafael, and Novato. These cities were exposed to varying types of growth pressures, and used different methods to control the quantity and quality of new development within their borders. Examined in the book are the direct effects of land use regulations (such as subdivision requirements, fees and charges, and the costs of delay) on new housing costs, and the effect of indirect factors (such as market readjustments, spillovers, and supply restrictions) on housing costs. The author concludes by suggesting ways by which we can limit the inflationary effect of land use controls while at the same time providing for a well-planned environment.

Dowall, David E. and Jesse Mingilton, *Effects of Environmental Regulations on Housing Costs*, Council of Planning Librarians, Bibliography #6, May 1979.

This is an annotated bibliography published by the Council of Planning Librarians. The bibliography is broken into three parts: a narrative summary of the literature, the annotated bibliography, and an extensive bibliography. The relevant research has been divided into three broad categories: descriptive, case studies, and econometric studies. The authors conclude, on the basis of the literature, that increased land use and environmental regulation have contributed to the rapid acceleration of housing costs. This is a useful source of information, and should be consulted early in the research process.

Einsweiller, Robert, "Increasing the Supply of Land in the Fringe Area," in HUD, *Reducing the Development Costs of Housing: Actions for State and Local Governments*, Proceedings of the HUD National Conference on Housing Costs, 1979.

This paper argues that supply should be seen as a dynamic, economic process and should be analyzed in relation to demand. Government should seek to manage a market, not implement a physical design and treat supply as a static, spatial concept. Nine causes of land supply problems are identified, and monitoring of developable land supply and sales price is proposed so that the supply/demand interaction is made clear to policy makers. The author admits that knowledge of exactly how to monitor is still somewhat sparse.

Gleeson, Michael E., "The Effects of an Urban Growth Management System on Land Values," Hubert Humphrey Institute of Public Affairs, Research Applied to National Needs Program, National Science Foundation, 1978.

This case study of the growth management system in Brooklyn Park, Minnesota found that the segmentation of land into developable and undevelopable portions produced sizable differences in the estimated market value per acre between developable and undevelopable portions. More than ⅔ of the cost differential was found to be due to the segmentation of the market.

Landis, John, "Land Regulation, Market, and Housing Price Inflation: Lessons from Three California Housing Markets," *APA Journal*, forthcoming.

The author describes four types of housing markets—perfectly competitive, contestable, imperfectly contestable, and closed. Three California housing markets—San Jose, Sacramento, and Fresno—are examined in the context of the author's typology. The major conclusion of this study is that the greatest price effects of local land use controls may be due to the restriction of the level or quality of the housing supply. In addition, the structure of the homebuilding industry is important in determining housing market effects of land use controls.

Nelson, Arthur, "Evaluation of Urban Containment Programs," PhD dissertation, published by the Center for Urban Studies, Portland State University, 1984.

This is a theoretical treatment of the effects of market segmentation associated with the Urban Growth Boundary (UGB) in the state of Oregon. A case study of Salem, Oregon is also included. The author theorizes that market segmentation should be detectable as a gap in the locus of land values at the UGB. Specifically, the land value gradient outside of the UGB should be convex because agricultural land values will decline with decreasing distance from the UGB as urban externalities increasingly inhibit agricultural productivity.

Schwartz, Seymour, "The Effect of Growth Management on Housing Prices: Methodological Issues and a Case Study," *Land Policy and Housing*, Lincoln Institute of Land Policy, Cambridge, Mass., 1981.

The author describes several methodological problems often found in studies looking at the effect of growth management on housing prices. A case study analysis of the effects of the Petaluma, CA, growth management system on housing prices is included, and examined using three different analytical models. The author explains the advantages and disadvantages of each of these analytical models. Finally, several methods by which the results in growth control studies can be strengthened are discussed.

Segal, David and Philip Srinivasn, "The Impact of Suburban Growth Restrictions on U.S. Housing Price Inflation 1975-1978," unpublished, July 1980.

This empirical study uses two stage least squares regression on a cross section of 51 metropolitan areas. One of the major sources of housing inflation is shown to be a variable reporting suburban growth restrictions—the fraction of potentially developed land just beyond the margin of urban settlement that is 'sequestered' from growth. Suburban growth restrictions explained as much as 40% of the variation in urban housing price inflation unexplained by demand side factors (income, population changes, mortgage rate increases). The impact of growth restrictions on housing costs was found to be curvilinear.

Seidel, Stephen R. *Housing Costs and Government Regulations: Confronting the Regulatory Maze*, The Center for Urban Policy Research, 1978.

This empirical study examines the effect of government regulation on housing costs. The regulations examined were building codes, energy-conservation measures, subdivision requirements, zoning controls, growth controls, environmental controls, and financing mechanisms. Three types of regulation costs were identified: direct costs, the costs of delay and uncertainty, and the costs of unnecessary or excessive requirements. The article is focused on the effects of regulation, but does not specifically examine the effects of a decrease in residentially-available land supply on housing costs.

Urban Land Institute and Gruen, Gruen & Associates, "Effects of Regulation on Housing Costs: Two Case Studies," 1977.

The relationship between government regulation and housing inflation is explored using case studies of San Jose, CA, and Jacksonville, FL. The relationship was found to be dependent on two main items: whether government regulation actually restricted available land supply, or increased development costs without restricting supply; and the elasticity of demand for housing. In San Jose, where supply was restricted and demand was relatively inelastic, 20-30% of housing cost increases resulted directly from local growth management policies.

Witte, Ann, "An Examination of Various Elasticities for Residential Sites," *Land Economics*, 53, 4, 1977.

This article examines the price elasticity of demand for single family sites. Price elasticity is shown to depend, among other things, on the number and closeness of available substitutes. The extent to which other submarkets are viewed as suitable substitutes by housing purchasers will act to increase elasticity and reduce potential increases in price in the first submarket.

The "Market Factor" and Excess Supply

Several growth management programs have attempted to allot a quantity of unrestricted land supply which is above that projected for development in a designated time period. The calculation of this "market factor" (how much available land should be allotted over and above projected demand so that the housing market can operate effectively without inflation?) is the subject of the reports and articles in this section.

Hoben, James, "Determining the Appropriate Level of Urban Land Supply," *Land For Housing: Developing a Research Agenda*, Report 85-3, Lincoln Institute for Land Policy, Cambridge MA, February 1985.

This descriptive article examines considerations which should be part of calculations of available land supply quantity. Technical considerations will often be part of calculating what supply and demand ratios will preserve competitive non-inflationary land markets. The ratio of buildable land to demand required to ensure competitive market will likely vary with rate of growth and the specific submarket. Time frame and geographical context for the supply/demand ratio are also important to consider. Finally, information on land prices for representative parcels is strongly recommended as a factor in determining an appropriate supply of available urban land.

Metropolitan Council of the Twin Cities Area, "Development Framework Policy, Plan, Program," 1975.

Within each of eight sectors within the Urban Service Area, a sufficient supply of land was planned for public services to meet the projected demand plus 5 additional years of urbanization. The purpose of the 5-year surplus was to dampen any tendencies toward land price inflation. This system permitted free choice over the general location for development within a sector, while at the same time permitting the government reasonable control over the cost of regional public services.

Montgomery County (Maryland) Planning Board, "Land Supply and Demand—Sixth Growth Policy Report," November 1980.

The MCPB found no normative standard for determining the correct ratio of land supply to market demand so as to provide sufficient market flexibility. The Board felt that the absolute supply of land for each residential dwelling unit type is important to detail, but land prices can still increase because the supply of a certain type of housing potential is concentrated in a few geographical areas. Location, structure type, density, and ownership are all factors which can be used to judge the "adequacy" of the vacant land supply.

Portland Metropolitan Service District, "Urban Growth Boundary Findings," 1979.

The MSD, in defining the Urban Growth Boundary, allocated a land supply 15% over and above projected demand through the year 2000. The land market was assumed to not be affected in the future by an UGB which includes a 15% market factor. There was no breakdown of the UGB into sectors in applying this market factor.

Monitoring—Objectives and Important Concepts

Dowall, David E., "Reducing the Cost Effects of Local Land Use Controls," *APA Journal*, April 1981.

This article provides guidance to those jurisdictions wishing to monitor their land supplies. Recommended land market attributes which should be monitored include: acres of existing land uses by category/location, inventory of raw and vacant land by location, determination of developable land (raw land minus land with physical or environmental constraints) in the jurisdiction categorized by availability of services, potential number of residential lots (based on zoning or intensity constraints) classified by service availability, and estimate of expansion of public services per year, and number of lots added to supply. In addition, monitoring should be spatially disaggregated according to distinct land or housing submarkets. The author notes that setting a land monitoring system in operation will require a "substantial commitment from local planners and elected officials."

People for Open Space, "A Resource Manual on Assessing Residential Land Availability," Technical Memo #2, 1983 (512 Second St., San Francisco, CA. 94107).

A helpful guidebook which examines the different ways "availability" of land can be defined, the techniques that can be used to inventory vacant land, the information sources available on vacant land, and the treatment of "underutilized" land. Land supply surveys done for six urban areas in California and Oregon are described in order to show the varying methods and techniques used in land supply inventories. People for Open Space is a non-profit conservation organization concerned with the regional planning and open space needs of the San Francisco Bay region.

Real Estate Research Corporation, *Infill Development Strategies*, published by APA Planners Press and Urban Land Institute, 1982.

As part of its analysis of infill development opportunities, this book discusses the advantages and limitations of each of the possible sources of data concerning vacant land supply. Tax assessor's records, aerial photos, land use and zoning maps, and field surveys are examined.

Systems in Use: Characteristics

Allen, Susan, "A Land Supply and Demand Monitoring System for King County, Washington," in Black, Thomas and James Hoben (eds.), *Urban Land Markets: Price Indices, Supply Measures, and Public Policy Effect*, ULI Research Report #30, 1980.

The author is former chief planner and manager of the growth management plan for King County, Washington (Seattle area). This article is a thorough examination of the King County system from its origin in 1977 through 1980. Especially helpful are the sections on system limitations and suggested improvements. Although the King County system has evolved since 1980, this article should be helpful to those jurisdictions wishing to start a monitoring system or encountering problems during the first few years of implementation.

Ameele, Noel, and Gary Zouzoulas, "Systems Support for Land Use Planning in San Jose, CA," unpublished, 1982/3.

The authors are Senior Planner and Information Systems Coordinator for San Jose, respectively. This practical paper outlines the evolution of the San Jose system from mainframe to microcomputer to minicomputer-based. The paper also discusses the importance of making an aggressive effort to quantify the benefits of a monitoring system in a cost effectiveness analysis. Three types of benefit dollars are discussed: cost displacement, cost avoidance, and value added.

Bartlett, Ray, "Developable Land Supply and Demand Monitoring Systems in the Portland Metropolitan Area," in Black, Thomas, and James Hoben (eds.), *Urban Land Markets: Price Indices, Supply Measures, and Public Policy Effect*, ULI Research Report #30, 1980.

As of 1980, the author was an economist with the Metropolitan Service District in Portland, Oregon. The article discusses the land inventory of the 4-county area done in 1977. The author states that the non parcel-specific nature of the database hurt the credibility and perception of the system by political decision-makers and the private sector. The land inventory was based on the census tract, not the parcel, as the basic unit of tabulation. The increased specificity of the 1979 update increased the usefulness of the system, but it also complicated the updating task. The author recommends tying the system into tax assessor's records, and making use of geocodes when recording land use data.

Gruen, Gruen & Associates, "LandTrak: The Tri-Valley Land Use Database," unpublished, 1985.

This short descriptive paper discusses the computerized monitoring system currently being developed by GG&A, a planning consulting firm based in San Francisco. Data at the parcel level may be grouped into four categories: physical characteristics, demographic links (at census tract level), location within jurisdictions and service areas, and development potential (based on General Plan designation and development approval status). The hardware is a super-micro, and the software is a relational database manager.

Hysom, John, and Stephen Ruth, "A Nationwide Assessment of Local Government Planning Information Systems," Center for Real Estate and Land Use Analysis, School of Business Administration, George Mason University, Fairfax, Virginia, October 1983.

This paper has two distinct parts. The first gives a general description of the Urban Development Information System (UDIS) of Fairfax County, Virginia. The second part discusses the results of the George Mason University Questionnaire Survey of 1983, whose purpose was to find out how successful was the technology transfer of the HUD-sponsored UDIS. Of 80 cities and counties responding to the survey, 72 (or 90.0%) had either a complete or partial computerized information system, or were developing one. The most common applications of computerized information systems in planning were: 1) parcel inventory, 2) building permit tracking, 3) building inspections, and 4) rezoning applications.

Munson, Michael, "Twin Cities Metropolitan Area Land Inventory and Analysis," in Black, Thomas, and James Hoben (eds.), *Urban Land Markets: Price Indices, Supply Measures, and Public Policy Effects*, ULI Research Report #30, 1980.

The author is Program Manager for Research on the Metropolitan Council of the Twin Cities Area. This article discusses the monitoring system of the Metro Council. The system's basic data source has been aerial photos augmented by building permit data and field checks. The inventory is recorded in tables by municipality and planning area districts. The most crucial concern of monitoring has been to provide insights into the development process so that forecasting capabilities can improve.

New Haven Office of Housing and Neighborhood Development, "Pilot Neighborhood Analysis: Using SOLIR Software Package," November 1983.

This paper discusses the use of computers by OHND prior to the implementation of their current monitoring system. SOLIR ("Small On-Line Research") software was used to store and statistically analyze data on properties. The software was used during a pilot neighborhood study of 8 neighborhoods, each described by 90 factors either transferred from existing mainframe tapes or manually inputted. OHND's satisfying experience with automation during this pilot study encouraged them to develop their monitoring system the following year.

New Haven Office of Housing and Neighborhood Development, "Managing Municipal Information Needs Using Micro-Computers: Conference Summary and Background Materials," October 4-5, 1984.

The first part of this report is a summary of the proceedings of the conference "Managing Municipal Information Needs" held in New Haven October 4-5, 1984. The panelists in the conference consisted of twelve experts with varied backgrounds in mainframe and microcomputers, database system development and management, policy-making and policy analysis. Major discussion issues are summarized along with responses to propositions distributed to panelists prior to the conference. The second part of the report is a description of the New Haven computerized system. The Land Use Information System (LUIS) is a microcomputer based system which allows the tracking of progress of both individual parcel-specific cases and entire government program activity. Two guidelines guided the development of the monitoring system: 1) each separate information element should be based on user needs, and 2) common parcel identifiers are essential to link separate elements. Appendices include a brief description of nine information systems in other cities. This report should be especially helpful to jurisdictions looking into the possibility of initiating a microcomputer-based information system.

People for Open Space, "A Resource Manual on Assessing Residential Land Availability," Technical Memo #2, 1983.

People for Open Space is a non-profit conservation organization primarily concerned with the regional planning and open space needs of the San Francisco Bay region. This guidebook discusses the different methodologies and data sources used in five land supply surveys done in California and Oregon. The surveys were done by ABAG (Association of Bay Area Governments), San Mateo County (CA), Novato city (CA), San Jose (CA), and 1000 Friends of Oregon. The appendices include sample survey forms from these areas.

Real Estate Research Corporation, *Infill Development Strategies*, published by APA Planners Press and Urban Land Institute, 1982.

A good source of information on four county/regional and seven municipal monitoring systems. For each inventory, such items as objectives, data sources, coverage, information collected, updating, costs, and dissemination are documented. The eleven monitoring jurisdictions are: Twin Cities Metro Council, Miami Valley Regional Planning Council, Lane County (OR), Portland MSD, King County (WA), Denver, Wilmington (DE), Washington, D.C., Toledo, Dallas, and Milwaukee.

Monitoring Systems Outside the United States

Canada Mortgage and Housing Corporation, Land and Infrastructure Division, "The Land and Infrastructure Mapping Program," January 1980.

Spurr, Peter, "The Canadian Land and Infrastructure Mapping Program," in Black, Thomas, and James Hoben (eds.), *Urban Land Markets: Price Indices, Supply Measures, and Public Policy Effects*, ULI Research Report #30, 1980.

Both papers describe the CMHC's Land and Infrastructure Mapping Program, and are similar in detail. One or the other should suffice for the interested reader. The Program is interesting because it is a federal government service which provides all governments with information regarding suburban land supply. It started in 1974, and is currently operating in 27 of Canada's largest urban regions. The program is operated by CMHC, but the entire database and summary analysis are reproduced and shared with municipal and provincial governments. Another interesting aspect of the program is that it is a manual system. The database covers the principal features of land supply: infrastructure, all zoned undeveloped lands, all proposed subdivisions, all unbuilt subdivisions, and all developer holdings. Each parcel is classified according to its various planning and servicing characteristics, and parcels are organized in sectors (usually municipalities or subregional planning areas).

Home, Robert, "Information Systems for Development Land Monitoring," *Cities*, November 1984.

An interesting discussion of land resource registers and land monitoring systems which exist in England. Joint land availability studies are now required by law. Local planning authorities are required to collaborate with private homebuilders in preparing these studies. Other registers focus on housing, industrial land, vacant land, and derelict land. The author also discusses 4 monitoring systems which exist in England. Conclusions in the article include the following. Development of monitoring systems in England has been uneven, with occasional retreats from such systems due to financial constraints and operational difficulties. Active agencies in the field of land monitoring have usually been motivated by one of the following: severe development pressures combined with local land shortages, opportunities presented by creation of new authorities, political commitment to public control of land resources, pilot schemes encouraged by central government, and particular interests and expertise of officers.

Research Centre for Urban and Regional Planning (Delft, The Netherlands), "The SALADIN System: A Spatially Oriented Information System for Planning and Management," August 1985.

The Spatial Analysis and Automatic Data Processing Information System was developed by the national government of the Netherlands. It uses the city block as the basic unit of tabulation and is composed of three major parts: a geographic base file (GBF) of digitized segments, administrative data files and statistics linked to GBF by data entry procedures, and computer programs which combine data from the GBF and administrative files to produce table listings and thematic maps. The system is designed as an interactive package on microcomputers. The most significant benefits are related to the following applications: network analysis and shortest path finding, neighborhood relations, catchment areas and analysis, impact allocation and analysis, overlay processing, and updating of spatial cross-reference files.

The Computer and Local Government: Implementation Considerations, Effects on Inter-Agency Relationships, Effects on Policy-Making

There is a growing literature on the role of computers in local government, and no attempt is made here to canvass that literature. What follows should provide the reader with a starting point for research on the role of computers in government.

Dueker, Kenneth J., "An Approach to Integrated Information Systems for Planning," in Kraemer, Kenneth L. and John L. King (eds.), *Computers in Local Government: Urban and Regional Planning*, Auerbach Publishers, 1980 (with supplements).

The author is Director, Center for Urban Studies, Portland State University. This article examines four subsystems of an information system: management, data processing, data analysis, and information use. Few systems have paid much attention to a separate management function, although the author believes they should. Because of imprecise data requirements and ambiguous objectives, the "design of an information system for planning is more of an art than a science," and a systematic design is difficult to achieve. The pros and cons of comprehensive versus incremental system designs are discussed. It is felt that an incremental system design for planning is necessary to keep abreast of the fast-changing planning process. However, systems designers should be able to limit options and debates regarding the system design.

Horwood, Edgar M., "Planning Information Systems: Functional Approaches, Evolution, and Pitfalls," in Kraemer, Kenneth L. and John L. King (eds.), *Computers in Local Government: Urban and Regional Planning*, Auerbach Publishers, 1980 (with supplements).

The author is Director, Urban Data Center, University of Washington, Seattle. This article examines 5 generic planning functions (as identified by Martin Meyerson in 1956) as providing a framework for linking information systems with planning. The author sees the 1960-1980 period as a "para-automation" period having a series of independent information automation thrusts. The 1980's is seen as a decade of database and data management development for multipurpose use. The article concludes with a discussion of the pitfalls and cautions associated with automated information systems in government.

Huxhold, William E., "Planning Agencies and the Data Processing Department: Working Together Effectively," in Kraemer, Kenneth L. and John L.

King (eds.), *Computers in Local Government: Urban and Regional Planning,* Auerbach Publishers, 1980 (with supplements).

The author is Project Director, Policy Development Information Systems, Milwaukee. This article focuses on organizational problems often associated with the interaction between planning and data processing departments which often impede effective computer use for planning purposes. These factors include different goals, different modes of operation, unrealistic expectations from both parties, lack of communication, and organizational restrictions. Tools available for improving organizational cooperation include: organizational changes, technological innovations, personnel development, and management planning.

Huxhold, William E., "Automated Systems for Building Permits Processing and Housing Code Inspection Reporting," in Kraemer, Kenneth L. and John L. King (eds.), *Computers in Local Government: Urban and Regional Planning,* Auerbach Publishers, 1981 (supplement).

This article discusses the advantages and implementation considerations associated with an automated building permit tracking subsystem. The database should consist of information from the application (owner's name, premise address) and final inspections record (completion date, disposition code), and should be geocoded to the census tract or other appropriate subarea. The advantages of automated public information recordkeeping and retrieval are increased government efficiencies and increased availability of the information to the public.

Kraemer, Kenneth L., "The Politics of Model Implementation," *Systems, Objectives, Solutions,* 1981.

This interesting article discusses a multi-stage process of implementation of computerized decision support systems: *Introduction*—system considered for adoption and some early pilot testing; *Adaptation*—broader support is developed, further instruction and training; *Incorporation*—system no longer appears as new innovation, becomes part of common activities of organization. The author uses a case study of a computerized fiscal impact model of Irvine, California to more clearly define these stages. One of the author's conclusions is that, in a political environment, an automated system's symbolic value can be as important as its substantive value to policy makers.

Stern, Robert A. and Nancy Stern, *Computers and Information Processing* (2nd ed.), Wiley and Sons, New York, 1985.

This textbook is recommended for those who feel uncomfortable or overwhelmed with the ideas and terminology of computer information systems. The book's chapters are clearly laid out, with outlines and good introductions preceding each chapter. An especially helpful chapter is one dealing with the different modes of data processing (centralized, distributed, decentralized).

URISA, "Papers from the Annual Conferences of the Urban and Regional Information Systems Association," 1962-1985.

The Urban and Regional Information Systems Association is the largest and oldest organization focusing on the effective and efficient use of information systems technology in the public sector. Invited papers to the annual conferences are published and are an essential source of information on a wide variety of topics concerning information systems. The membership is comprised primarily of administrators, professionals, and technical staff officers from local governments. Members' interests include: government functions and public sector applications, hardware and software configurations, database development, intergovernmental relations, and public/private cooperation in the use of information systems. Published proceedings are available through the Secretariat, URISA, 1340 Old Chain Road, Suite 300, McLean, Virginia 22101.

Glossary

Batch Processing: the processing of data in groups or batches at fixed intervals, as opposed to the continuous processing of data. Files that are maintained using batch processing techniques are actually current only at the time at which they are updated. Contrast with on-line.

Buildout: the total potential number of dwelling units or residents in an area based on current zoning or general plan designation.

Centralized data processing: the performance of the data processing function by a single computer center within an organization. Contrast with decentralized and distributed data processing.

Chaining: a method of linking records in a relational database.

Database manager: software package designed to provide users with a fully integrated management information system. A database management system includes techniques for creating, updating, and querying files, as well as reporting on file information.

Data capture screen: the organization of the database so as to facilitate the entering, updating, and accessing of information. ALSIS will be most useful to users if data capture screens are tailored to the needs of the individual user departments. A planning data capture screen, for example, would be set up so as to present the user with only that information which is entered by or relevant to the planning department.

Decentralized data processing: use and control of independent data processing facilities by individual departments within an organization. Each department controls its own processing needs, and there is no central library computer facility. Contrast with centralized and distributed data processing.

Digitize: in computer mapping, to express or represent in a digital form data that are not discrete data, such as the boundaries of a polygon. To establish X-Y coordinates for map boundaries.

Distributed data processing: method of processing designed to incorporate the benefits of both centralized and decentralized data processing. This form combines a central library computer with the ability to download subsets of the full database to individual workstations in user departments. Some definitions of "distributed" include all forms of remote-access systems. In this report, we define "distributed" systems more inclusively to be those where both access and processing is distributed. Contrast with centralized and decentralized data processing.

Download: to electronically transfer all or some data from a mainframe or minicomputer to a microcomputer. One of the features of distributed data processing.

Field: a group of consecutive storage positions within a computer record used to represent an item of data. Examples of fields within a record include owner's name, parcel number, and so on.

File: a collection of individual computer records that is treated as one unit. A parcel file, for example, refers to an agency's complete collection of parcel records.

Geo-coding: providing data elements in a parcel record to identify the parcel in geographic space. Address and Census Tract are two commonly used geocodes.

Graphics: refers to a mode of computer processing and output in which a significant part of the output information is in pictorial form. The information may range from a simple histogram or other plot to a complex map annotated with alphanumerics and displayed in color. Often, graphics refers solely to the plotting of information and not to the mapping.

Grid: a square or rectangular form of standard, repeated representation used to subdivide computer maps into small areas. It is incapable of capturing irregular features to be mapped because of its rigid form. Contrast with polygon.

Hardware: physical equipment used in data processing, as opposed to programs, procedures, rules, and associated documentation.

Hardwiring: linkage by cable of an input/output device, such as a terminal, to a central processing unit. With hardwiring, telephone lines are not necessary for transmitting messages from a remote location to a central processing unit.

Hierarchical: a method of organizing data so that major items are grouped together, then subdivided into minor ones.

Interactive: application in which each entry calls forth a response from a system or program, as in an inquiry system. Implies a continuous dialog between the user and the system.

Mainframe computer: traditional computer system used for 1) information processing in centralized or distributed mode, and 2) data communications applications where terminals at remote locations transmit data to a central processing unit.

Mapping: mode of computer processing which displays digitized X-Y coordinates in pictorial form. Computer maps are often annotated with alphanumerics and displayed in color.

Menu-driven: software which displays a list of available machine functions for selection by the operator. Especially beneficial to those users unfamiliar with the database contents or with computer operations generally.

Microcomputer: a computer system whose processing unit is a microprocessor. A basic microcomputer includes a microprocessor, storage, and a input-output facility, which may or may not be on one chip.

Minicomputer: a computer that does not need the closely controlled environment of mainframe computers, and has a richer instruction set than that of a microprocessor.

Modem: a device that converts digital data signals so that they can be transmitted over communication lines; an abbreviation for modulator-demodulator. Allows computers to communicate over telephone lines.

Network analysis: computer programs often used for determining the optimal location of future public infrastructure, based on constraints and the locations of existing infrastructure.

On-line: system where the input data enters the computer directly from the point of origin and/or the output data is transmitted directly to where it is used; all equipment within a computer operation is hooked up directly to the central processing unit.

Overlay: to compare two different types of data for a particular area by superimposing one on top of the other. Often used in computer mapping of environmental factors/variables to come up with a description of the mapped area based on the combination of overlay data types.

Password security: allows only certain users to access and/or update system information.

Pipeline: development ongoing or in the initial stages of approval. Usually consists of projects under construction, subdivisions, rezonings, and special permits.

Polygon: a form of representation used in digitizing computer maps that can exactly follow property lines and geographic features. It is more flexible than grid representation in capturing irregular features to be mapped.

Relational: type of database organization where records which have common attributes are linked to one another using chains and pointers. Facilitates searches and sorts.

Record: a set of related fields treated as a unit. A parcel record, for example, consists of fields relating to a particular parcel.

Screen: generally, the surface of a cathode-ray tube on which information can be displayed; more specifically, to select and display information in response to an instruction or an inquiry.

Software: internal computer programs or routines professionally prepared to simplify programming and computer operations.

Spreadsheet: programming package that enables people to make projections and to build models. Ideal tool for forecasting, financial analysis, inventory analysis, and budget preparation.

Statistical package: a set of subroutines written for collecting, summarizing, analyzing, and interpreting variable numerical data.

Terminal: a device, usually equipped with a keyboard and display device, capable of sending and receiving information over a link.

Terminal security: allows only certain terminals to retrieve system information. This form of security is used predominantly to secure confidential information.

Update security: the strongest security of the three (terminal and password are the other forms). Allows only certain data elements to be updated or modified by specified persons. Updater has to first be identified by terminal and password before update security comes into effect.

Vendor Software: standard computer programs or routines which are sold on the market by manufacturers. Examples include SAS (Statistical Analysis Service) and SPSS (Statistical Package for the Social Science) on the mainframe, Lotus 1-2-3 and R-base 5000 on the microcomputer.

About the Authors

David R. Godschalk is Professor of Planning at the University of North Carolina at Chapel Hill. Formerly Chairman of the UNC Department of City and Regional Planning and Editor of the Journal of the American Institute of Planners, Godschalk has practiced planning as Director of Planning for Gainesville, Florida, and as vice president of a Tampa planning consulting firm. He has done research and consulting on growth management, co-authored *Constitutional Issues of Growth Management* (APA Press, 1979), and served as peer reviewer of the 1984 Comprehensive Plan for Lee County, Florida. In addition to automated information systems, his current work focuses on development dispute resolution, negotiated development methods, and the use of development management for hazard mitigation. A registered architect as well as a planner, he holds a B.A. from Dartmouth, a B.Arch. from Florida, and an M.R.P. and Ph.D. from the University of North Carolina.

Scott A. Bollens is a Research and Teaching Assistant in the Department of City and Regional Planning at the University of North Carolina, where he is pursuing a doctoral degree in planning. His planning experience includes management of an environmental consulting firm in Santa Cruz, California, and work with the Santa Cruz County Planning Department and the John Muir Institute. His research activities include directing a telephone survey of hazard mitigation policies and practices under a National Science Foundation study of Hurricane Hazard Reduction, development of a computer-based spatial information and mapping system, and conducting a study of political and fiscal determinants of central city/suburb income inequality in 100 SMSA's. He is the 1985 recipient of the ASPA Graduate Student Award for Best paper on Intergovernmental Relations for his paper "An Intergovernmental Perspective on Special District Governments." Bollens holds a B.A. from UCLA and an M.R.P. from the University of North Carolina.

John S. Hekman is Associate Professor of Finance in the School of Business Administration at the University of North Carolina. His experience includes work as an economist with the Federal Reserve Banks of Boston and Atlanta, as an economics faculty member at Boston College, and as a research associate at the Harvard-MIT Joint Center for Urban Studies. His research has included studies of the office building construction cycle, the effect of environmental regulations on industrial development, the effect of family labor force participation on urban residential location, and the location of high technology industry. He has consulted with the North Carolina Department of Natural Resources and Community Development. Hekman teaches in the joint Planning/Business Administration graduate program in real estate and urban development at UNC. He holds a B.A. from Valparaiso University and an M.B.A. in Finance and a Ph.D. in Economics from the University of Chicago.

Mike E. Miles is Foundation Professor of Urban Development in the School of Business Administration at the University of North Carolina. His experience includes positions as Vice President of Finance with the Alpert Investment Corporation, as an accountant with Peat, Marwick, Mitchell & Co., and as an operations research analyst with NASA. He has directed the M.B.A. Program at UNC and the North Carolina Real Estate Research Center. He is co-author of *Modern Real Estate* (Wiley and Sons, second edition, 1984) and has written a number of cases and articles on real estate development. Miles co-directs the UNC joint graduate program in real estate and urban development. He is a Certified Public Accountant and a Senior Real Property Analyst, and has consulted with many national corporations. He holds a B.S. from Washington and Lee University, an M.B.A. from Stanford, and a Ph.D. from the University of Texas at Austin.